3 5/∞

W9-BVM-804

Modern Critical Interpretations

William Shakespeare's Richard III

Modern Critical Interpretations

These and other titles in preparation

William Shakespeare's
Richard III

Edited with an introduction by

Harold Bloom
Sterling Professor of the Humanities
Yale University

Chelsea House Publishers ◊ *1988*

NEW YORK ◊ NEW HAVEN ◊ PHILADELPHIA

© 1988 by Chelsea House Publishers, a division
of Chelsea House Educational Communications, Inc.,
  95 Madison Avenue, New York, NY 10016
  345 Whitney Avenue, New Haven, CT 06511
  5068B West Chester Pike, Edgemont, PA 19028

Introduction © 1985 by Harold Bloom

Printed and bound in the United States of America

10 9 8 7 6 5 4 3 2 1

∞ The paper used in this publication meets the minimum
requirements of the American National Standard for
Permanence of Paper for Printed Library Materials,
Z39.48–1984.

Library of Congress Cataloging-in-Publication Data
William Shakespeare's Richard III / edited and with an
introduction by Harold Bloom.
    p. cm.—(Modern critical interpretations)
  Bibliography: p.
  Includes index.
    Contents: Dream and plot / Marjorie B. Garber—
Shakespeare's halle of mirrors / Michael Neill—Neither
mother, wife, nor England's queen / Madonne M. Miner—The
dead-end comedy of Richard III / John W. Blanpied—Military
oratory in Richard III / R. Chris Hassel, Jr.—Usurpation,
seduction, and the problematics of the proper / Marguerite
Waller—Savage play in Richard III / C. L. Barber and Richard
P. Wheeler.
    ISBN 0–87754–937–0 (alk. paper) : $24.50
    1. Shakespeare, William, 1564–1616. King Richard III.
    2. Richard III, King of England, 1452–1485, in fiction,
drama, poetry, etc. [1. Shakespeare, William, 1564–1616. King
Richard III.   2. Richard III, King of England, 1452–1485, in
fiction, drama, poetry, etc.   3. English literature—History
and criticism.]   I. Bloom, Harold.   II. Title: Richard III.
III. Series.
PR2821.W55 1988
822.3 3—dc19   87–17825

Contents

Editor's Note

This book brings together a representative selection of the best modern critical interpretations of Shakespeare's history play *Richard III*. The critical essays are reprinted here in the chronological sequence of their original publication. I am grateful to Cornelia Pearsall for her assistance in editing this volume.

My introduction briefly sets Richard in the context of the tradition he helped foster, that of the Jacobean hero-villain and his literary progeny down to our own time. Marjorie B. Garber begins the chronological sequence of criticism with a consideration of the various dreams in *Richard III*, remarking that while these dreams conform to the Renaissance idea that dreams are prophecies, they are also (especially Clarence's dream) psychologically sound.

The narcissistic imagery of mirrors is emphasized in Michael Neill's reading of Richard's character. Madonne M. Miner examines all of the play's female characters, analyzing their changing roles in the action, while John W. Blanpied presents *Richard III* as comedy gone wrong, as it were, while insisting that Buckingham is the true Machiavel, rather than Richard.

In an essay informed by Renaissance manuals on military oratory, R. Chris Hassel, Jr., contrasts Richard's and Richmond's speeches to their men before the battle of Bosworth. Marguerite Waller, setting deconstructive and feminist modes of reading against one another, achieves an original and compelling reading of the scene in which Richard's rhetoric seduces both Anne and himself.

In this book's final essay, the late C. L. Barber and Richard P. Wheeler set Richard both in his historical context and in the context of the tetralogy, examining Shakespeare's use of his sources in the play; they suggest that Richard's movement towards self-destruction is organized by a series of actions in which he cuts himself off from male fellowship.

Introduction

                                I
Why, I, in this weak piping time of peace,
Have no delight to pass away the time,
Unless to see my shadow in the sun
And descant on mine own deformity.
And therefore, since I cannot prove a lover
To entertain these fair well-spoken days,
I am determined to prove a villain
And hate the idle pleasures of these days.
                                      (1.1.24–31)

The opening ferocity of Richard, still duke of Gloucester, in *The Tragedy of Richard the Third* is hardly more than a fresh starting point for the development of the Elizabethan and Jacobean hero–villain after Marlowe, and yet it seems to transform Tamburlaine and Barabas utterly. Richard's peculiarly self-conscious pleasure in his own audacity is crossed by the sense of what it means to see one's own deformed shadow in the sun. We are closer already not only to Edmund and Iago than to Barabas, but especially closer to Webster's Lodovico who so sublimely says: "I limn'd this nightpiece and it was my best." Except for Iago, nothing seems farther advanced in this desperate mode than Webster's Bosola:

                        O direful misprision!
I will not imitate things glorious
No more than base: I'll be mine own example.—
On, on, and look thou represent, for silence,
The thing thou bear'st.
                                      (5.4.87–91)

   Iago is beyond even this denial of representation, because he does will silence:

1

> Demand me nothing; what you know, you know:
> From this time forth I never will speak word.
>
> (5.2.303–4)

Iago is no hero-villain, and no shift of perspective will make him into one. Pragmatically, the authentic hero-villain in Shakespeare might be judged to be Hamlet, but no audience would agree. Macbeth could justify the description, except that the cosmos of his drama is too estranged from any normative representation for the term hero-villain to have its oxymoronic coherence. Richard and Edmund would appear to be the models, beyond Marlowe, that could have inspired Webster and his fellows, but Edmund is too uncanny and superb a representation to provoke emulation. That returns us to Richard:

> Was ever woman in this humor woo'd?
> Was ever woman in this humor won?
> I'll have her, but I will not keep her long.
> What? I, that kill'd her husband and his father,
> To take her in her heart's extremest hate,
> With curses in her mouth, tears in her eyes,
> The bleeding witness of my hatred by,
> Having God, her conscience, and these bars against me,
> And I no friends to back my suit [at all]
> But the plain devil and dissembling looks?
> And yet to win her! All the world to nothing!
> Hah!
> Hath she forgot already that brave prince,
> Edward, her lord, whom I, some three months since,
> Stabb'd in my angry mood at Tewksbury?
> A sweeter and a lovelier gentleman,
> Fram'd in the prodigality of nature—
> Young, valiant, wise, and (no doubt) right royal—
> The spacious world cannot again afford.
> And will she yet abase her eyes on me,
> That cropp'd the golden prime of this sweet prince
> And made her widow to a woeful bed?
> On me, whose all not equals Edward's moi'ty?
> On me, that halts and am misshapen thus?
> My dukedom to a beggarly denier,
> I do mistake my person all this while!
> Upon my life, she finds (although I cannot)

Myself to be a marv'llous proper man.
I'll be at charges for a looking–glass,
And entertain a score or two of tailors
To study fashions to adorn my body:
Since I am crept in favor with myself,
I will maintain it with some little cost.
But first I'll turn yon fellow in his grave,
And then return lamenting to my love.
Shine out, fair sun, till I have bought a glass,
That I may see my shadow as I pass.

(1.2.227–63)

Richard's only earlier delight was "to see my shadow in the sun /And descant on mine own deformity." His savage delight in the success of his own manipulative rhetoric now transforms his earlier trope into the exultant command: "Shine out, fair sun, till I have bought a glass, / That I may see my shadow as I pass." That transformation is the formula for interpreting the Jacobean hero-villain and his varied progeny: Milton's Satan, the Poet in Shelley's *Alastor*, Wordsworth's Oswald in *The Borderers*, Byron's Manfred and Cain, Browning's Childe Roland, Tennyson's Ulysses, Melville's Captain Ahab, Hawthorne's Chillingworth, down to Nathanael West's Shrike in *Miss Lonelyhearts*, who perhaps ends the tradition. The manipulative, highly self-conscious, obsessed hero-villain, whether Machiavellian plotter or later, idealistic quester, ruined or not, moves himself from being the passive sufferer of his own moral and/or physical deformity to becoming a highly active melodramatist. Instead of standing in the light of nature to observe his own shadow, and then have to take his own deformity as subject, he rather commands nature to throw its light upon his own glass of representation, so that his own shadow will be visible only for an instant as he passes on to the triumph of his will over others.

Dream and Plot

Marjorie B. Garber

The great popularity of the dream as a dramatic device among the Elizabethans is surely due at least in part to its versatility as a mode of presentation. Both structurally and psychologically the prophetic dream was useful to the playwright; it foreshadowed events of plot, providing the audience with needed information, and at the same time it imparted to the world of the play a vivid atmosphere of mystery and foreboding. Thus the Senecan ghost stalked the boards to applause for decades, while the cryptic dumb show, itself a survival of earlier forms, remained as a ghostly harbinger of events to come.

Even in his earliest plays, Shakespeare began to extend and develop these prophetic glimpses, so that they became ways of presenting the process of the mind at work in memory, emotion, and imagination. What was essentially a predictive device of plot thus became, at the same time, a significant aspect of meaning. Dream episodes, in short, began to work within the plays as metaphors for the larger action, functioning at once as a form of presentation and as a concept presented. This is clearly the case with the dramatic action of *Richard III*. From Queen Margaret's curse to Clarence's monitory dream and the haunting nightmare of Bosworth Field, omen and apparition define and delimit the play's world.

The consciousness of dreaming which is to dominate the play throughout makes its first striking appearance in Richard's opening soliloquy:

From *Dream in Shakespeare: From Metaphor to Metamorphosis.* © 1974 by Yale University. Yale University Press, 1974.

> Plots have I laid, inductions dangerous,
> By drunken prophecies, libels and dreams,
> To set my brother Clarence and the king
> In deadly hate the one against the other.
>
> (1.1.32–35)

Dreams here appear in what will become a familiar context for the early plays, clearly analogous to "plots," "prophecies," and "libels" as elements of the malign irrational. Richard has deftly contrived to manipulate circumstance by preying upon the vulnerability of the superstitious king. Encountering his brother Clarence on his way to the Tower, he is told what he already knows: the king, says Clarence,

> harkens after prophecies and dreams,
> And from the crossbow plucks the letter G,
> And says a wizard told him that by G
> His issue disinherited should be;
> And, for my name of George begins with G,
> It follows in his thought that I am he.
>
> (1.1.54–59)

The poetry here halts and stammers, a mirror of the simplicity and confusion which make Clarence such an easy target. He considers himself a reasonable man, and, confronted by unreason, he is both impotent and outraged. Yet such an absolute rejection of the irrational is a fatal misjudgment in the world of *Richard III*, and Clarence's skepticism becomes a means to his destruction, just as later his determined denial of the truth of his own dream will lead directly to his death.

Here, in the first scene of the play, a sharp contrast is already apparent between the poles of dream and reason. Significantly, Richard, the Machiavel, defines himself as a realist, in contrast to the foolish Clarence and the lascivious Edward; he intends to control his fate and the fate of others through an exercise of reason. Yet the very first evidence of his supposed control, the false prophecy of "G," is truer than he knows: not George but Gloucester will disinherit Edward's sons. Clarence's passive skepticism about the irrational is but an image of Richard's more active scorn, and Richard's vulnerability to the powers of the imagination at Bosworth is prefigured by Clarence's prophetic dream of death.

The basic pattern of dream as prophecy is exemplified in simplest form by the dream of Lord Stanley as it is reported to Hastings in act 3:

He dreamt the boar had rased off his helm.
. . . .
Therefore he sends to know your lordship's pleasure,
If you will presently take horse with him
And with all speed post with him to the north
To shun the danger that his soul divines.

                                        (3.2.11,15–18)

But Hastings, like Clarence, reacts with instinctive disbelief:

Tell him his fears are shallow, without instance;
And for his dreams, I wonder he's so simple
To trust the mock'ry of unquiet slumbers.

                                        (3.2.25–27)

In the dream and its reception we have the fundamental design of early Shakespearean dream: the monitory dream which is true, but not believed. Stanley dreams that Richard—the boar—will cut off their heads, and Hastings rejects this suggestion absolutely. He reasons, further, that to react to it will have the undesirable effect of making the prophecy come true, since if it is known that they distrust him, Richard will give them reasons for distrust.

To fly the boar before the boar pursues
Were to incense the boar to follow us
And make pursuit where he did mean no chase.

                                        (3.2.28–30)

This is a politic and sophisticated conclusion; it is also a false one, and it places Hastings in the revealing category of those who scoff at omens. He is in fact a prisoner of his own reason. "A marvelous case it is," remarks Holinshed, with customary exactitude, "to hear either the warning that he should have voided or the tokens that he could not void." It is only hours later, when he hears himself condemned, that he at last grasps the enormity of his mistake.

For I, too fond, might have prevented this.
Stanley did dream the boar did rase our helms,
And I did scorn it and disdain to fly.
Three times today my footcloth horse did stumble,
And started when he looked upon the Tower,
As loath to bear me to the slaughterhouse.

                                        (3.4.80–85)

This belated account of an earlier omen, equally disregarded, establishes even more clearly Hasting's distrust of the entire realm of the irrational. It is only in the developing context of supernatural warnings that he, too late, can interpret the sign correctly.

For his part, Richard follows the same course with Hastings as he did with Clarence and Edward: he pretends to have discovered "devilish plots / Of damnèd witchcraft" (3.4.59–60), ostensible reasons for his own deformity, and condemns Hastings to death for his cautious skepticism. Once again, he employs witchcraft as a device, something to be used rather than believed in. Apparently, then, he and Hastings occupy positions at opposite ends of the rationalist scale: Hastings the victim, warned by true omens he chooses to ignore; Richard the victor, creating false signs and prophecies through which he controls the superstitious and the skeptical alike. Yet they are more alike than they seem at first. When Richard himself becomes the dreamer, the recipient of omens and supernatural warnings, his rationalist posture is susceptible to the same immediate collapse; the terrifying world of dream overwhelms him, as it has overwhelmed Clarence and Hastings, at the critical moment of his ill-starred defense on Bosworth Field.

The double dream at Bosworth is an apparition dream, related to the risen spirits in *2 Henry VI* and *Macbeth* as well as to the ghosts of *Hamlet* and *Julius Caesar*. Richard and Richmond, encamped at opposite ends of the field, are each in turn visited by a series of ghosts representing Richard's victims: Edward Prince of Wales, Henry VI, Clarence, Rivers, Gray and Vaughan, Hastings, the two young princes, Anne, and Buckingham. As each spirit pauses he speaks to Richard like a voice of conscience within the soul: "Dream on thy cousins smothered in the Tower" (5.3.152); "Dream on, dream on, of bloody deeds and death" (l. 172). And then, in a formal counterpoint, each turns to Richmond and wishes him well. The whole scene is symmetrically arranged, the contrast of sleeping and waking, despair and hopefulness, emphasized by the rigidity of the form. For Richard, "guiltily awake"(l. 147), this is the fulfillment of the last term of Margaret's curse:

> The worm of conscience still begnaw thy soul!
> Thy friends suspect for traitors while thou liv'st,
> And take deep traitors for thy dearest friends!
> No sleep close up that deadly eye of thine,
> Unless it be while some tormenting dream
> Affrights thee with a hell of ugly devils!
>
> (1.3.221–26)

Richard's sleeplessness, like Macbeth's, is the mark of a troubled condition of soul, the outward sign of an inward sin. Margaret in her self-chosen role as "prophetess" (1.3.300) has called it down upon him, adding yet another to the series of omens which culminate in dream.

The terror which this dream evokes in Richard's mind is explicitly shown in his frightened soliloquy ("Is there a murderer here? No. Yes, I am" [5.3.185]), and even more in his subsequent conversation with Ratcliff. "O Ratcliff," he exclaims, "I have dreamed a fearful dream!" This is a very different man from the bloodless Machiavellian who plants the seeds of Clarence's execution in his brother's brain. His cry is now the Shakespearean equivalent of Faustus's last speech:

> KING RICHARD: O Ratcliff; I fear, I fear!
> RATCLIFF: Nay, good my lord, be not afraid of shadows.
> KING RICHARD: By the apostle Paul, shadows tonight
> Have struck more terror to the soul of Richard
> Than can the substance of ten thousand soldiers.
>
> (5.3.215–19)

In his fear he hits the point precisely: the "shadows," because they arise from the symbol-making unconscious, are more threatening than the substance. The Richard who can say "Richard loves Richard: that is, I am I" (5.3.184) must create his own omens if they are to strike him with terror. Consciousness is the one enemy he can neither trick nor silence. From the controller of dreams he has become the controlled, the victim of his own horrible imaginings.

The Bosworth dream, like the predictive dream of Stanley, serves a structural purpose as well as a psychological one. The apparitions of murdered friends and kinsmen recall to the onlooker all the atrocities that have gone before, the perfidies of 3 Henry VI as well as the events of the present play. The device is dramatically useful because of the complexity of the historical events involved; many in the audience will probably not remember whose corpse is being mourned at the play's beginning, nor what relation the Lady Anne bears to the Lancastrian monarchy. Points of history are thus clarified at the same time that a psychologically convincing "replay" takes place in Richard's mind. The direct inverse of the prophetic dream, this recapitulation simultaneously furthers the ends of psychological observation, historical summation, and structural unity, so that the sequence of dreams and omens which are the formal controlling agents of Richard III are all embodied in the last revelation at Bosworth.

As useful a device as this final dream proves to be, it carries with it several inherent drawbacks. The apparatus of the serial ghosts is cumbersome and formal, analogous to (and probably derived from) the older pageantry of Deadly Sins and Heavenly Virtues. Holinshed, again a useful touchstone, describes the assemblage merely as "divers images like terrible devils" and rejects any supernatural interpretation: "But I think this was no dream but a punction and prick of his sinful conscience." His eagerness to moralize causes him to miss a more significant point: the very equivalence of *dream* with "the punction and prick of conscience" goes deep into the structural and psychological roots of the play. But Holinshed's devils are simply punishment figures of a generalized and abstract sort; by replacing them with the pageant of Richard's victims seeking retributive justice, Shakespeare transforms the entire significance of the last dream. He will use such a formal array only once more, in the series of apparitions which address Macbeth on the heath. There, again, the ghostly figures will become part of the king's private and terrible mythology of symbols, at the same time that they recall the ominous, monitory procession of deadly sins common to Tudor drama.

But the interior world of dream in *Richard III* was to undergo yet another alteration and expansion, quitting the specific formalism of the Bosworth dream for a freer and richer exploration of the subconscious. Just as Richard's apparent control of "prophecies, libels, and dreams" was abruptly replaced by subjugation to internal terrors, so, in Clarence's dream, imagination and the creative unconscious begin to replace the mechanism of witchcraft and omen as the proper architects of dream. Clarence's prophetic dream falls into three structurally distinct parts, each of which is important to the pattern of dream use in the play. The first part (1.4.9–20) recounts his supposed sea journey with Gloucester, their reminiscences of the wars, and Gloucester's accidental fall:

> As we paced along
> Upon the giddy footing of the hatches,
> Methought that Gloucester stumbled, and in falling
> Struck me (that thought to stay him) overboard
> Into the tumbling billows of the main.
>
> (1.4.16–20)

There is both psychological and symbolic truth in this passage. What Freud called the "dream-work," the process by which the latent dream thoughts are transformed into the manifest dream content, has rendered Clarence's latent suspicion of Richard, a suspicion he finds emotionally unbearable, into more reassuring terms. The subconscious thought "Gloucester wants to murder me," rejected by the conscious, here appears in the disguised form "Gloucester will kill me by accident, though he doesn't want to." Outwardly, of course, this prediction falls into the category of monitory dreams, the "tumbling billows of the main" anticipating the butt of malmsey in which Clarence is to be ingloriously drowned. We may, if we choose, regard it solely as another ignored or misunderstood omen, a class for which there is precedent in Shakespeare's works and in those of his contemporaries. But the passage, like the play, offers more than one possibility. While it fits into the pattern of unheeded warnings, it also begins to become an intrinsic part of the mind of the speaker, communicating to us something even he himself does not know.

Gloucester "stumbles" metaphorically in seeking the crown. This information is conveyed more directly in his own words; his soliloquies are psychological revelations, his disappointments and ambitions shown in psychological terms. He is a wholly new kind of character in Shakespeare, and we are able to follow the workings of his mind in a wholly new way. When he thinks aloud at the close of *3 Henry VI*, "Clarence, beware. Thou keep'st me from the light" (5.6.84), he gives to us the same warning which is given in Clarence's dream. And though we enter Clarence's consciousness only once, in the dream itself, it is clear that some part of him suspects what we know to be a certainty: Richard's design on his life. To read the accident passage as merely another foreshadowing is to ignore the remarkably acute psychology with which the poet approaches the unique occasion of the dream. Through the dream device he permits us to enter Clarence's consciousness for a moment, in the same way we have entered Richard's. This is why the dream appears so different in style and imagery from anything else in the play. The latent suspicion Clarence harbors is authentically presented in masked form by his subconscious mind. And what is most interesting is that the process of masking here takes the form of *metaphor*.

The mention of the "tumbling billows" meantime precipitates the dream into its second phase, the lyrical description of a world undersea. The chief characteristic of this vision—for that is what it really appears to be—is a striking contrast of mortality and eternity, the obscenely decaying body and the insensate but highly valued jewels which endure unchanged.

> A thousand men that fishes gnawed upon;
> Wedges of gold, great anchors, heaps of pearl,
> Inestimable stones, unvalued jewels,
> All scatt'red in the bottom of the sea.
>
> (1.4.25–28)

The ambiguity in "unvalued" is key to the whole. To Clarence in the extremity of his fear the jewels, though priceless, are without value as compared to human life. "Some lay in dead men's skulls," he continues,

> and in the holes
> Where eyes did once inhabit there were crept,
> As 'twere in scorn of eyes, reflecting gems
> That wooed the slimy bottom of the deep
> And mocked the dead bones that lay scatt'red by.
> (1.4.29–33)

What is chiefly remarkable about this image is its sheer physicality, the fascinated horror of a man contemplating his own imminent death. When the same image next appears in Shakespeare, it will have been curiously purified of passion:

> Those are pearls that were his eyes:
> Nothing of him that doth fade,
> But doth suffer a sea change
> Into something rich and strange.
> (*Tempest*, 1.2.401–4)

In Ariel's song mortality has become immortality, the eyes not replaced by pearls but transformed into them. The difference between this view and Clarence's suggests the direction in which vision and dream will develop in the plays. In *Richard III*, however, the undersea passage is nightmare to the dreamer, though its language is touched with a strange and haunting lyricism.

The passage which succeeds it, by contrast, is vividly dramatic, working through dialogue rather than through images. Two spirits appear to Clarence and confront him with his crimes, much as Richard's victims do on Bosworth Field. The tradition here evoked is that of the underworld visit of classical epic, the dead man greeted by the shades of those he knew on earth.

> I passed, methought, the melancholy flood,
> With that sour ferryman which poets write of,
> Unto the kingdom of perpetual night.
> (1.4.45–47)

Here is yet another sea journey, parallel to the channel crossing of the dream's first section. This generally unnoticed parallel is significant, for it again utilizes authentic dream logic to clarify the total meaning of the dream. In the first sea journey, as we have seen, Clarence overtly ascribes the cause of his fall to accident, though he betrays a latent distrust of his brother Richard. Here, in the second journey, he pictures his destination as hell, and supplies vivid reasons—in the forms of Warwick and Edward, prince of Wales—why he deserves damnation. The displaced figure of the stumbling Richard is strongly related to Clarence's assessment of his own guilt: he has perjured himself (i.e., dissembled about his allegiance) and slain the heir to the throne. But Richard, too, is a perjurer and will become a murderer; he has had Clarence falsely imprisoned and has then pretended ignorance and concern over the event; he will later have him killed because he stands in the line of succession. Clarence thus displaces his unacceptable distrust of Richard, by transferring his just suspicions to analogous episodes in his own life. Simultaneously he punishes himself for having these suspicions by turning them against himself. The ghosts of Warwick and Edward thus possess a multiple significance for the dream's meaning, establishing even further the psychological accuracy of its form.

The more direct significance of these figures is of course historical recapitulation, as it will be in the Bosworth dream. The magnificent tongue twister of a line,

> "What scourge for perjury
> Can this dark monarchy afford false Clarence?"
> (1.4.50–51)

is meant to recall the elaborate chain of events by which, in *3 Henry VI*, Clarence first pledges his support to Warwick and then deserts him. On that occasion Warwick rebukes him as a "passing traitor, perjured and unjust" (5.1.106), and the charge is repeated by the prince of Wales: "Thou perjur'd George," he taunts (5.5.34), and when Clarence joins with his brothers to stab the prince to death, he does so in a spirit of resentment as well as anger, retorting, "there's for twitting me with perjury" (l.40). The accusations made by the ghosts in his dream are thus authentic reminders of Clarence's history. The prince's ghost resembles the accusatory apparitions of Bosworth, but is much more closely assimilated into the consciousness of the dreamer:

> A shadow like an angel, with bright hair
> Dabbled in blood, and he shrieked out aloud,
> "Clarence is come, false, fleeting, perjured Clarence,
> Seize on him, Furies, take him unto torment!"
> (1.4.53–57)

This is no ceremonial intoning, but rather a visionary visitation. The prince is not identified by name, but is only presented in fragmented detail, as if hastily glimpsed—"a shadow like an angel," "bright hair," "blood." We are inside the mind of Clarence, and we see the ghost through his eyes. In keeping with the play's general design, the ghosts of Clarence's mental landscape appear only secondhand, as related through his dream. It is Richard's consciousness with which we are continually in contact, and only Richard's ghosts make actual appearances on stage.

Yet there is something extremely important about the relationship of Clarence's vision of Warwick and Edward to the actual ghosts of act 5. Clarence's dream internalizes the ghosts, portrays them directly as elements of imagination. Gone is the cumbersome apparatus of the Bosworth dream, and gone likewise is the aura of artificiality created by the mechanical pattern of omen and fulfillment. Dream here is an agency of liberation, a means of freeing prophecy from device and relating it to psychological intuition. Imagery bears a bigger part, and association is legitimately employed to make images into symbols. The materials of Clarence's dream are still embryonic, and its technique stands in marked contrast to that of the rest of *Richard III*. But it is the first real anticipation of a new use of dream, to be refined and expanded in the later plays.

Shakespeare's Halle of Mirrors: Play, Politics, and Psychology in *Richard III*

Michael Neill

> *Here the King is, in the first half of the tragedy, the mastermind of the Grand Mechanism, a demiurge of history.*
>
> Jan Kott

> *God in love with His own beauty frames a glass, to view it by reflection.*
>
> Thomas Vaughan

Richard III is the most stridently theatrical of all of Shakespeare's plays. The superb histrionic insolence of Richard, his stagy relish in confidential soliloquy and aside, is matched by a self-conscious patterning of plot, spectacle, and language, as if Shakespeare's artistry were being flaunted like Richard's own. And the connection is insistently underlined by the use of stage metaphors: poet, actor, and protagonist unite in a Marlovian pageant of self-display. This ostentatious theatricality, while it has a lot to do with the play's continuing success on the stage, has presented critics with problems almost as intractable as those faced by Sir Laurence Olivier when he attempted to translate *Richard* into the alien conventions of cinema. E. A. J. Honigmann, prefacing his recent edition of the play, shows a characteristic unease about its Senecan melodrama and the rhetorical rigidities which embody a "primitive" psychological technique working "at a level not much superior to that of *The Spanish Tragedy*." Criticisms of this sort may seem inevitable if *Richard III* is placed beside *Macbeth*, the mature tragedy which it most obviously anticipates, and no one would contest the

From *Shakespeare Studies* 8 (1975). © 1975 by the Council for Research in the Renaissance.

fact that the style of the early histories is incapable of "the intellectual and emotional insights of the tragic period." Nevertheless, what is impressive about *Richard III* is the dramatic intelligence with which Shakespeare makes his limitations work for him, and this is an aspect of the play which can be brought out if one thinks of *Richard III* less as an immature version of the pathological horrors of *Macbeth* and more as a preliminary investigation of ontological problems like those explored in *Hamlet*.

At first sight the connection between *Hamlet* and *Richard III* may seem tenuous. It does, however, occur to Honigmann himself, who writes of Richard's "curious, inverted affinity to the Prince of Denmark, the other Shakespearean hero with a connoisseur's sense of theatre." Anne Righter similarly sees *Richard III* as being "like Hamlet . . . a tragedy filled with assertions of the actor's power," to the point that Richard himself emerges "more as an example of the power wielded by the actor than as a figure of treachery and evil." And Jan Kott's essay on the histories, operating from very different premises, insists on the necessity of interpreting *Hamlet* in the light of *Richard III* and *Richard III* in the light of *Hamlet*.

Richard's confidence in the efficacy of acting as a mode of action certainly stands at the opposite pole from Hamlet's metaphysical agonies, but it, too, is the product of something much deeper than mere connoisseurship—just as Shakespeare's own assertions of the actor's power are more than an extravagant mannerist flourish. Hamlet sets out to obey the philosopher's precept "know thyself," and the play is about the vertiginous terrors concealed by that deceptively simple injunction. Richard, with none of Hamlet's moral sensibility, but poised on the edge of the same ontological abyss, sets out, rather, to *create* himself. His methods are those of the theater. Crucial to both plays is the familiar quibble on "acting" and "action": it is through action that we realize what we are; it is through acting that we make real what we are not. Trapped by his awareness that this apparently absolute distinction is, in existential terms, unviable, Hamlet finds significant action impossible. He can redeem himself only by an act of nominalist faith, a magical proclamation of his selfhood—"This is I, Hamlet the Dane"—a proclamation that works only because it is rooted in a larger faith that makes the quest for intellectual self-knowledge an irrelevance. Richard begins and ends with a similar proclamation of his integral selfhood—"I am myself alone;" "Richard loves Richard: that is, I am I." But the blasphemous self-sufficiency of his "I am" belongs to the rhetoric of despair. The tragic paradox of Richard's position is that only action can validate the self he proclaims; and yet just because that self can be located only in action—because it is otherwise null, a chaos, unformed and un-knowable—action must take the form of acting, must become a way not of proving but of concealing the self, the void at the center of being. And when the external motives for action are removed, "Richard," literally, disintegrates.

I

Of course, both the metaphors which invite us to view historical events in a theatrical perspective and the characterization of Richard as a diabolic actor-hypocrite have a basis in the traditional materials on which Shakespeare was building. The world of *Richard III* is figured as a Wonderful Theater of God's Judgments, and men are depicted as mere puppet-actors, their movements dictated with a nice regard for witty symmetry by the Cosmic Ironist. Margaret, the furious prophetess, is the Chorus for His tragedy of blood. In act 4, scene 4, which she describes as a "dire induction" to a tragedy (ll. 5–7), she recalls the murder of her son Edward as a "frantic play," with Hastings, Rivers, Vaughan, and Grey as its sadistic audience (ll. 68–69); and she goes on to type the reign of Edward of York as a kind of May Game pageant, with Elizabeth as a Summer Lady:

> I call'd thee then vain flourish of my fortune;
> I call'd thee then poor shadow, painted queen,
> The presentation of but what I was;
> The flattering index of a direful pageant;
>
> . . . .
>
> A queen in jest, only to fill the scene.
>
> (4.4.82–91)

The impotence she ascribes to the pageant-actors is confirmed by the Duchess of York's abstraction of herself as "Woe's scene"—a passive spectacle of grief (l. 27). And that image in turn looks back to Elizabeth's sorrow at her Edward's death:

> DUCHESS: What means this scene of rude impatience?
> QUEEN ELIZABETH: To make an act of tragic violence.
>
> (2.2.38–39)

Though she sees herself as the maker of her own play, the best that Elizabeth and her fellow mourners can do is to compose an inert tableau of grief in a pageant they cannot direct:

> QUEEN ELIZABETH: Ah for my husband, for my dear Lord
>   Edward!
> CHILDREN: Ah for our father, for our dear Lord Clarence!
> DUCHESS: Alas for both, both mine, Edward and Clarence!
> QUEEN ELIZABETH: What stay had I but Edward? and he's gone.
> CHILDREN: What stay had we but Clarence? and he's gone.
> DUCHESS: What stays had I but they? and they are gone.
> QUEEN ELIZABETH: Was never widow had so dear a loss.
> CHILDREN: Were never orphans had so dear a loss.
> DUCHESS: Was never mother had so dear a loss.

(2.2.71–79)

Those who fancy themselves as directors of the theatrical procession find themselves in turn caught up in its inexorable movement. Hastings rejoices in the downfall of the queen's party in 3.2—"I live to look upon their tragedy" (l. 59)—but before two scenes are out, the plot has come full circle: "They smile at me who shortly shall be dead." (3.4.107). Death changes partners in a dizzy reel: God calls the tune. Buckingham, envisaging heaven as no more than the auditorium for God's brutal theater of revenge (5.1.3–9), squarely confronts its terrible ironies:

> That high All-Seer, which I dallied with,
> Hath turn'd my feigned prayer on my head,
> And given in earnest what I begg'd in jest.
> Thus doth he force the swords of wicked men
> To turn their own points in their masters' bosoms.

One thinks of Beard's Marlowe, gouging his own eye with the hand of blasphemy.

A God of the kind implied by these play metaphors will do well enough for a Puritan fanatic like Thomas Beard or a propagandist like Halle, and his activities accord with the providential scheme defined by Tillyard. But he presents problems for a dramatist—witness the didactic clumsiness of *The Atheist's Tragedy*. Seen from the viewpoint of Shakespeare's supposed "official self," the play belongs to an impressive but drastically limited kind of ritual theater, plotting the ironic symmetries of providence with equally exact schemes of action, spectacle, and rhetoric. The limitations are both moral and dramatic. Moral, because providence too easily appears, if not a mere instrument of human faction, then a model for its vicious plots; dramatic, because in denying the possibility of significant moral activity, it tends to reduce human action to a meaningless writhing.

Of course, Richmond's triumph appears to give official endorsement to this grand scheme—it could hardly do otherwise. But the play's total poetic statement is another matter. It is significant that the most humanly moving of Margaret's speeches is not among the cursings by which she marks the progress of nemesis but is her agonized questioning of the whole fatal process in act 1, scene 3:

> Did York's dread curse prevail so much with heaven
> That Henry's death, my lovely Edward's death,
> Their kingdom's loss, my woeful banishment,
> Should all but answer for that peevish brat?
> Can curses pierce the clouds and enter heaven?
>
> (1.3.190–94)

By the end of the scene she has convinced herself otherwise:

> I will not think but they ascend the sky,
> And there awake God's gentle-sleeping peace.
>
> (1.3.286–87)

But even here the violent yoking of gentleness and savagery creates an ambiguity. The endless spectacle of death glutting on life can hardly be other than sickening, and Margaret's question forces us to ask by what scale God distributes justice—if indeed He concerns Himself with it at all. Elizabeth's despairing retort to Richard in act 4, scene 4 suggests a heaven which denies justice to the victim, just as it cuts the oppressor from the sun:

> What good is cover'd with the face of heaven,
> To be discover'd, that can do me good?
>
> (4.4.240–41)

It is as though God (at best) has withdrawn His light from the fallen world and left it for the devil, Richard, to bustle in.

What finally raises the play's theater of revenge above mere ritual is the character of Richard himself—dramatist, producer, prologue, and star performer of his own rich comedy.

II

The way in which the character of Richard is developed out of a combination of More's Machiavellian "deep dissimuler" with the self-delighting witty Vice of the Moralities is perceptively traced by Anne Righter in her section on "The Legacy of the Vice." Here I am concerned with the surprising psychological insights which Shakespeare manages to produce from the manipulation of such thoroughly traditional material. Because the shaping of Richard's character is a process substantially begun in *3 Henry VI*, any full account of it must take that play into account, although *Richard III* as a dramatic structure is perfectly able to stand on its own.

Richard's delight in his prowess as an actor, the bustling energy of his performances, makes him in a sense the only lively moral positive in the play. His most sustained virtuoso exercise comes in the second scene, where it is tellingly placed against the embodiment of orthodox virtue—a corpse—the "poor, key-cold figure of a holy king" whom even Margaret recalls contemptuously as "Holy Harry" (4.4.25). Clearly it was this quality of style in Richard—what Honigmann calls his "glamour"—which attracted the citizen's wife to Burbage, and has excited audiences ever since. It's the same quality that stirs us in a Barabbas, a Volpone, or a Vindice. Just as it is the quality which wins Anne herself, who falls to Richard precisely because she is *not* deceived, because (as he intends) she is bowled over by the nerve, the *sprezzatura*, of the performance itself:

> Arise, *dissembler!* Though I wish thy death,
> I will not be thy executioner.
> (1.2.184–85; italics mine)

What is perhaps less obvious is the subtle psychological realism which lies behind the compelling staginess of Richard's character: the way in which his titanism is shown as the reflection of a most appalling emotional weakness and deformity.

Two important soliloquies in *3 Henry VI* contain all that is necessary for the development of Richard's character in the last play of the sequence. Like most of Richard's monologues, both take the form of extended asides to the audience, and both are ostensibly expressions of his naked, all-consuming ambition. But, in fact, they are much more than merely signposts to the plot. In the first (3.2.124ff.), Richard sketches the development of his ambition in a pseudodialectical form: too many lives stand between him and the crown he desires, and therefore he would be wiser to direct his energies to private satisfactions; but his physical ugliness appears to make this gratification of sexual lust a vanity even more absurd than lust for dominion, so that he is forced back again on his political aspiration. Trapped in this logical impasse, he concludes that the politician's formula of violence masked by smooth deceit offers his best release. The structure of Machiavellian rationalism is not, however, sufficient to contain the confused emotional impulses behind the speech. Richard broods obsessively on the theme of sexual love and his own deformity, the whole speech grows out of his bitter reflections on Edward's carnal prodigality, and one senses that the means of the curse he invokes—the grotesque tortures of syphilis—are imaginatively more important than its ends: to open Richard's pathway to the crown. The wanton multiplication of claimants to the throne—"Clarence, Henry, and his son young Edward, / And all the unlook'd-for issue of their bodies" (ll. 131–32)—is as much an affront to his sexual capacity as to his ambition. He posits an alternative to political enterprise only to provide an excuse for further masochistic flagellation. The unstable combination of self-pity, savage irony (tending always towards brutal self-parody), and an almost masturbatory relish in his own wickedness becomes the keynote of Richard's descants on his own deformity:

> Well, say there is no kingdom then for Richard;
> What other pleasure can the world afford?
> I'll make my heaven in a lady's lap,
> And deck my body in gay ornaments,
> And witch sweet ladies with my words and looks.
> O miserable thought! and more unlikely
> Than to accomplish twenty golden crowns!
> Why, love forswore me in my mother's womb;
> And for I should not deal in her soft laws,
> She did corrupt frail nature with some bribe,
> To shrink mine arm up like a wither'd shrub,
> To make an envious mountain on my back,
> Where sits deformity to mock my body;
> To shape my legs of an unequal size,
> To disproportion me in every part,
> Like to a chaos, or an unlick'd bear-whelp
> That carries no impression like the dam.
>
> (3 Henry VI, 3.2.146–62)

It is the strident self-assertion of an ego monstrously enlarged to protect an inner self pitiably warped and enfeebled. Physical deformity is felt as the outward manifestation of an inner formlessness, a mirror of psychological chaos. And the ontological vacuum is located in a profound emotional alienation: Richard cannot know himself because he cannot love himself, and he cannot love himself because he has never been loved—"love forswore me in my mother's womb." It is not only in a physical sense that Richard resembles the unlicked bear-whelp "that carries no impression like the dam": his relation with his mother, whose loathing is displayed with admirable economy in *Richard III*, has failed to provide Richard with the necessary locus for his sense of self.

The second of the two *3 Henry VI* soliloquies returns to this theme of love and maternal alienation:

> Indeed 'tis true that Henry told me of;
> For I have often heard my mother say
> I came into the world with my legs forward.
> . . . .
> The midwife wonder'd and the women cried,
> "O, Jesus bless us, he is born with teeth!"
> And so I was, which plainly signified
> That I should snarl, and bite, and play the dog.
> Then since the heavens have shap'd my body so,
> Let hell make crook'd my mind to answer it.
> I have no brother, I am like no brother;
> And this word "love," which greybeards call divine,
> Be resident in men like one another,
> And not in me: I am myself alone.
>
> (*3 Henry VI*, 5.6.69–83)

Richard here conceives of love in the terms set out in Ficino's *Commentary on Plato's Symposium*:

> Likeness generates love. Similarity is a certain sameness of nature in several things. If I am like you, you are necessarily like me; therefore, the same similarity which compels me to love you, forces you to love me. . . . Moreover, a lover imprints a likeness of the loved one upon his soul, and so the soul of the lover becomes a mirror in which is reflected the image of the loved one. Thereupon, when the loved one recognises himself in the lover, he is forced to love him.

Ficino, significantly, insists on love as a mode of self-realization: "When you love me, you contemplate me, and as I love you, I find myself in your contemplation of me; I recover myself, lost in the first place by [my] own neglect of myself, in you, who preserve me. You do exactly the same in me. . . . I keep a grasp on myself only through you as a mediary" (2.8). And the highest form of self-realization is naturally through love of God, of which all other loves are but shadows: "we shall seem first to have worshipped God in things, in order later to worship things in God; and shall seem to worship things in God in order to recover ourselves above all, and seem, in loving God, to have loved ourselves" (6.19). Love, the creative mirror by which we realize ourselves, has been withdrawn from Richard. A child, says D.W. Winnicott, "needs one person to gather his bits together," a mirror to establish his sense of integral identity; Richard, the unlicked bear-cub, carries no impression like his dam and so identifies his self as a chaos. Without form he can be "like" no one, and no one can be "like" him: he is "himself alone," with all the horror of isolation which that arrogant despair implies.

In the prologue-soliloquy with which he opens *Richard III*, Richard plays again on the theme of physical deformity and emotional alienation:

> But I, that am not shap'd for sportive tricks,
> Nor made to court an amorous looking-glass;
> I, that am rudely stamp'd, and want love's majesty
> To strut before a wanton ambling nymph;
> I, that am curtail'd of this fair proportion,
> Cheated of feature by dissembling nature,
> Deform'd, unfinish'd, sent before my time
> Into this breathing world, scarce half made up,
> And that so lamely and unfashionable
> That dogs bark at me as I halt by them—
> Why, I, in this weak piping time of peace,
> Have no delight to pass away the time,
> Unless to see my shadow in the sun
> And descant on mine own deformity.
>
> (1.1.14–27)

The glass which Richard mockingly rejects is the old icon of vanity, displaying the narcissistic image of the physical self. But since the body in turn is only an image or shadow of soul and mind, the inner self, the icon also doubles as an emblem of self-knowledge. And one is aware that Richard is as much concerned with psychological reality as with physical appearance. The solution to his anguish is a paradoxical one: "to see my shadow in the sun, / And descant on mine own deformity." He makes himself into a kind of travesty Narcissus, creating a false self to be the object of his consuming need for love. Ficino's account of Narcissus is helpful:

> A certain young man, Narcissus, that is the soul of bold and
> inexperienced man, does not see his own countenance, he never

notices his own substance and virtue, but pursues its reflection in the water, and tries to embrace it; that is, the soul admires the beauty in the weak body, an image in the flowing water, which is but the reflection of itself. It deserts its own beauty and never catches its shadow.

(6.17)

Richard's narcissism is in fact precisely a strategy to avoid the contemplation of his own true countenance. He sublimates his tearing consciousness of inner formlessness by concentrating on its outward image, which he creates as something outside himself, a shadow. Like an actor's shadow-self, it is a role whose recognition involves no necessary acknowledgment of self-knowledge, being part of the self-consciously adopted persona of a Machiavellian villain:

> And therefore, since I cannot prove a lover
> To entertain these fair well-spoken days,
> I am determined to prove a villain
> And hate the idle pleasures of these days.
> (1.1.28–31)

It is a characteristic of Richard's mode of histrionic self-consciousness that he regards even the wicked self concealed by his pious performances as itself a role, something to be "played":

> And thus I clothe my naked villainy
> With odd old ends stolen forth of holy writ,
> And seem a saint, when most I *play* the devil.
> (1.3.335–37; italics mine)

And the broad element of self-caricature, which is never more apparent than when he is ostensibly laying himself naked—"dogs bark at me as I halt by them"—is a reflection of this self-divisive strategy.

III

In that long soliloquy from *3 Henry VI* where Richard contemplates his own chaos, he imagines his political struggle in terms which powerfully suggest his agony of psychological confusion:

> And I—like one lost in a thorny wood,
> That rents the thorns, and is rent with the thorns,
> Seeking a way, and straying from the way

> Not knowing how to find the open air,
> But toiling desperately to find it out—
> Torment myself to catch the English crown;
> And from that torment I will free myself,
> Or hew my way out with a bloody axe.
>
> (*3 Henry VI*, 3.2.174–81)

The implication of self-division in the self-torment, and of self-destruction in the self-division, unconsciously anticipates the horrors of Richard's last night at Bosworth Field. And the method by which he proposes to end his torment is also, ironically enough, a method of self-division:

> Why, I can smile, and murther whiles I smile,
> And cry "Content" to that which grieves my heart,
> And wet my cheeks with artificial tears,
> And frame my face to all occasions.
>
>   .   .   .   .
>
> I can add colors to the chameleon,
> Change shapes with Proteus for advantages,
> And set the murtherous Machevil to school.
>
> (*3 Henry VI*, 3.2.182–93)

It is the method of the actor—a creator of multiple selves—and it is as an actor that Henry contemptuously sees him—"What scene of death hath Roscius now to act?" (*3 Henry VI*, 5.6.10). On the level of simple plot Richard emerges as the perfect actor-hypocrite, identifying himself in the last scene of *3 Henry VI* with the archetypal figure of Judas:

> To say the truth, so Judas kiss'd his master,
> And cried "All hail!" when as he meant all harm.
>
> (*3 Henry VI*, 5.7.33–34)

In *Richard III* we are constantly being reminded of Richard's theatrical virtuosity in perhaps a dozen different roles, by his self-congratulatory asides, by the games he plays with Buckingham, and even by the extravagant energy of the performances themselves, his sensuous delight in histrionic rhetoric:

> Because I cannot flatter and look fair,
> Smile in men's faces, smooth, deceive, and cog,
> Duck with French nods and apish courtesy,
> I must be held a rancorous enemy,
> Cannot a plain man live and think no harm,

> But thus his simple truth must be abus'd
> With silken, sly, insinuating Jacks?
>
> (1.3.47–53)

In one sense, of course, Richard's flair makes him only the most accomplished performer in a court of hypocrites, as the pageant of dissimulation in 2.1 shows. Indeed, the logic of political corruption ensures that the
self-division of hypocrisy is paralleled beyond the court: in the First Murderer's denial of conscience—"My voice is now the King's, my looks my
own" (1.4.170)—and in the pathetic evasions of Brakenbury and the
Scrivener:

> I will not reason what is meant hereby,
> Because I will be guiltless from the meaning.
>
> (1.4.93–94)

> Who is so gross
> That cannot see this palpable device?
> Yet who['s] so bold but says he sees it not?
>
> (3.6.10–12)

The scrivener's death warrant, beautifully engrossed for an execution
which has already taken place, is an epitome, at once horrible and absurd,
of a political charade in which all become passive, but nevertheless guilty,
actors. All, that is, except Richard. For what gives him his demonic power
is the way in which he seizes the freedom which an actor's function nor-
mally denies. The selves he creates are, or (at least until act 4) appear to
be, independent of any plot-mechanism but those which he himself de-
vises; and, more than that, they are actually agents in determining the roles
others must perform within his plots.

The prologuelike speech with which Richard opens his play, summa-
rizing previous action and outlining the shape of that to come, creates for
him a kind of extradramatic status which is borne out in his running commentary of asides through the first four and a half acts. In the speech itself
the presenter-function is conflated with that of a playmaker:

> *Plots* have I laid, *inductions* dangerous,
> By drunken prophecies, libels, and dreams,
> To set my brother Clarence and the King
> In deadly hate the one against the other.
>
> (1.1.32–35; italics mine)

The puns are appropriate both because, until the end of 4.3, the plot of the play is virtually indistinguishable from Richard's plotting and because his characteristic way of working out his plots is theatrical: consequently, the action tends to resolve itself into a series of plays within the play with Richard as author-actor. ("The Loving Brother," "The Loyal Friend," "The Witty Lover," "The Loyal Subject," "The Good Protector," "The Reluctant Prince," "The Bluff Soldier"—to name only some of the most obvious. Cf. Sanders). Of these, the most breathtaking is that with Anne in 1.2, the play of "The Witty Lover."

The purpose of playing, as Hamlet tells us, is to hold a mirror up to nature, and Richard's theatrical magic works by mirrors. Hamlet's performance for Gertrude in the closet scene sets up a glass to show her her inmost self; Richard's performance for Anne works by more confusing sleights. If there seems to be something unconvincingly histrionic about Anne's first two big speeches, we soon find out why. Seeming to accept her role of grief-enraged wife and daughter, Richard draws Anne through a mirror-maze of stichomythia, where speech reflects speech in apparently innocent antithesis for eighty lines, until she is made to feed him precisely the cue he wants:

> ANNE: Out of my sight, thou dost infect mine eyes!
> GLOUCESTER: Thine eyes, sweet lady, have infected mine.
> ANNE: Would they were basilisks, to strike thee dead!
>
> (1.2.148–50)

Disastrously—but inevitably—her gibe recalls a thousand Petrarchan clichés on the killing beams of the lady's eyes, and it enables Richard to slip into the full routine of the rejected lover. By a further mirror-trick his speech becomes an inverted image of her opening salvo of curses: the revenge invoked then is offered her now—but in terms which render it farcically irrelevant. Anne may have his life, but only if she consents to close his play in a final tableau of the cruelty of love: the earthly Venus plunging her sword into the humble heart of her servant. And yet, in the rhetorical labyrinth into which she has wandered, the only conceivable alternative is the grant of mercy:

> GLOUCESTER: But shall I live in hope?
> ANNE: All men, I hope, live so.
> [GLOUCESTER:] Vouchsafe to wear this ring.
> [ANNE: To take is not to give.]
>
> (1.2.199–202)

However she looks, Anne finds her image fatally defined in the mirrors of Richard's art: a looking glass world in which joke becomes reality and reality a player's sour jest, where Anne's curses reflect back, as Richard has mockingly warned (l. 132), upon herself—

> If ever he have wife, let her be made
> More miserable by the [life] of him
> Than I am made by my young lord and thee!
>
> (1.2.26–28)

—where Margaret in turn will be made to curse herself, Hastings to pronounce his own sentence of death, and the citizens of London to implore a tyrant's accession.

Act 1, scene 2 ends as it began, in monologue—Richard's epilogue balancing Anne's prologue. And in this concluding flourish of the theatrical mirror, Richard himself returns to the icon of the looking glass:

> My dukedom to a beggarly denier,
> I do mistake my person all this while!
> Upon my life, she finds (although I cannot)
> Myself to be a marv'llous proper man.
> I'll be at charges for a looking-glass
> And entertain a score or two of tailors
> To study fashions to adorn my body:
> Since I am crept in favor with myself,
> I will maintain it with some little cost.
>
> . . . .
>
> Shine out, fair sun, till I have bought a glass,
> That I may see my shadow as I pass.
>
> (1.2.251–63)

The scene we have just witnessed has been just such a glass. For if its immediate end has been the conquest of Anne, its true purpose, like all of Richard's performances, has been to reflect, and to realize, himself—to call a self into being out of the nothing, the chaos within: "And yet to win her! All the world to nothing!" (1.2.238). The shadow of his nothing falls upon all that is.

The sun which Richard invokes is the heraldic sun of York, but it is also the sun of majesty in whose light he may cast his long shadow upon the world, a world which will thus become a gigantic reflector of his own reality. And at a further remove it may suggest the Sun of Divinity, which his shadow seems to cut from the world, Plato's inner light on which all human understanding and commerce depends:

The sun generates eyes and it bestows upon them the power to see. This power would be in vain, and would be overwhelmed by eternal darkness if the light of the sun were not present, imprinted with the colours and shapes of bodies. . . . In the same way, God creates the soul and to it gives mind, the power of understanding. The mind would be empty and dark if it did not have the light of God, in which to see the principles of everything.

(Compare the exchange with Margaret, 1.3.263–75:

> GLOUCESTER: Our aery buildeth in the Cedar's top and dallies
>   with the wind and scorns the sun.
> QUEEN MARGARET: And turns the sun to shade-alas, alas!)

The suggestion somberly deepens the resonances of his threat to Clarence at the end of *3 Henry VI*:

> Clarence, beware! thou [keep'st] me from the light,
> But I will sort a pitchy day for thee.
>
> (*3 Henry VI*, 5.6.84–85)

Clarence's death in act 1, scene 4 is made into a grotesque mirror image of the sacrament with which he entered the world, the symbolism of rebirth horribly realized in a literal new-christening in the Tower. So that the golden time of Richard, the third sun of York, becomes the reign of a terrible Antichrist:

> For thou hast made the happy earth thy hell,
> Fill'd it with cursing cries and deep exclaims.
>
> (1.2.51–52)

> KING RICHARD: And came I not at last to comfort you?
> DUCHESS: No, by the holy rood, thou know'st it well,
>   Thou cam'st on earth to make the earth my hell.
>   A grievous burthen was thy birth to me,
>   Tetchy and wayward was thy infancy.
>
> (4.4.165–69)

Not only does Richard appear as an antitype of the Comforter, but also as a kind of travesty Creator, making a new earth in the image of his own deformity, like the clumsy and malign demiurge of Gnostic myth. In Platonic accounts of creation, God, "in love with his own beauty, frames a glass to view it by reflection"; that glass is the universe:

The desire of a thing for the propagation of its own perfection is a kind of love. Absolute perfection consists in the supreme power of God. This perfection the divine intelligence contemplates, and hence the divine will desires to generate the same perfection beyond itself; because of this love of propagation everything was created by Him.

And it is this creation by love which gives the world its coherent order:

If Love creates everything, He also preserves everything, for the functions of creation and preservation always belong together. Certainly like things are preserved by like, and moreover, Love attracts the like to the like. Every part of the earth, joined by mutual love, links itself with other parts of earth like itself.

(3.2)

Richard's creation by hate, on the other hand, can only be a creation of disorder: a mirror of his own psychological chaos. Where Love joins the universe together in mutual attraction—"a circle of good, revolving from good to good perpetually"—Richard's self-propagating "I am" sets up an apparently endless cycle of division in which "sin will pluck on sin" (4.2.63) as "wrong hath but wrong, and blame the due of blame" (5.1.29), a cycle through which the desperate incoherence of Richard's inner state is at last resolved in annihilating self-division—"Myself myself confound!" (4.4.399)—the serpent of evil gnawing at its own tail.

IV

Richard's kingdom is built "on brittle glass" in more than the sense he intends at 4.2.60. It is a kingdom of mirror-plays and actor-shadows in which he manipulates the lens. Mirror images register in the consciousness of other characters, too, but purely as metaphors for passive observation and reflection, metaphors which tend by their stylized remoteness to suggest an impoverishment of human relations. For Anne, the corpse of her father-in-law is contracted to a kind of mirror-emblem:

If thou delight to view thy heinous deeds,
Behold this pattern of thy butcheries.

(1.2.53–54)

For the bereaved Duchess of York, her dead sons are recalled as reflections of their father; and Richard, seen as a distorting mirror of these dead, is also a reflector of her own shame:

> I have bewept a worthy husband's death,
> And liv'd with looking on his images;
> But now two mirrors of his princely semblance
> Are crack'd in pieces by malignant death,
> And I for comfort have but one false glass,
> That grieves me when I see my shame in him.
>
> (2.2.49–54)

Shadows, shades, ghosts, and finally distorted reflections—the living are only images, good and bad, of the dead, or (more accurately) of one's own passion of loss.

The way in which relationships are reduced to mere perspectives of solipsist mirrors in this corrupted world is powerfully dramatized in certain "mirror scenes," notably 2.2 and 4.4. In the antiphonal patterns of the language (and in the staging such patterns appear to invite) one grief reflects another in apparently infinite recession. Elizabeth, for Margaret in 1.3, is merely a spurious image of herself, the true queen—"Poor painted queen, vain flourish of my fortune!" (l. 240); by 4.4, Elizabeth, Margaret, and the Duchess of York have become exact mirror-images of one another's sorrow:

> QUEEN MARGARET: [Tell over your woes again by viewing
> mine:]
> I had an Edward, till a Richard kill'd him;
> I had a [Harry], till a Richard kill'd him:
> Thou hadst an Edward, till a Richard kill'd him;
> Thou hadst a Richard, till a Richard kill'd him.
> DUCHESS: I had a Richard too, and thou didst kill him;
> I had a Rutland too, thou [holp'st] to kill him.
> QUEEN MARGARET: Thou hadst a Clarence too, and Richard
> kill'd him.
>
> (4.4.39–46)

"Shadow," "presentation," "pageant," "dream"—the terms of Margaret's speech beginning at line 82 point to the way in which the fantasies of the glass have become reality. But the elaborate parallelism asserts the identity of their situations only, since the formalism denies any identity of feeling,

any sympathy. Their relationship is displayed as a mere epitome of the re-
morseless mechanical formula by which human lives are organized in the
first tetralogy—"wrong hath but wrong, and blame the due of blame."

Perhaps the most terrible of the play's mirror figures appears in the
complex symbolism of Clarence's dream; cast haphazard among the other
emblems of mortal vanity are jewels:

> Some lay in dead men's skulls, and in the holes
> Where eyes did once inhabit, there were crept
> (As 'twere in scorn of eyes) reflecting gems,
> That woo'd the slimy bottom of the deep,
> And mock'd the dead bones that lay scatt'red by.
>
> (1.4.29–33)

It is as though the eyes, travestying their traditional function as "windows
of the soul," have become mere mirrors, at once mocking their owners'
humanity and denying the possibility of communication with that humanity. The image anticipates Buckingham's irony in the council scene—

> We know each other's faces; for our hearts,
> He knows no more of mine than I of yours,
> Or I of his, my lord, than you of mine.
>
> (3.4.10–12)

—and Richard's subsequent rejection of Buckingham:

> none are for me
> That look into me with considerate eyes.
>
> (4.2.29–30)

Buckingham—"respective," "circumspect,"—attempts to see beyond the
mirrors, and dies for it.

Clarence's gems reflect only the slimy bottom of the deep upon itself,
as Richard's mirror-play ultimately shows Anne only the image of her
own corruption. Her eyes which pour their balm on Henry's wounds and
which she repeatedly tries to make reject the image of Richard—"mortal
eyes cannot endure the devil" (1.1.45) and "Out of my sight! Thou dost
infect mine eyes" (1.2.148)—becomes the metaphorical agents of her fall,
as Richard's verbal mirror turns her rhetoric back upon herself:

> GLOUCESTER: Thine eyes, sweet lady, have infected mine.
> ANNE: Would they were basilisks, to strike thee dead!
> GLOUCESTER: I would they were, that I might die at once;

For now they kill me with a living death.
Those eyes of thine from mine have drawn salt tears,
Sham'd their aspects with store of childish drops:
These eyes, which never shed remorseful tear—
No, when my father York and Edward wept
To hear the piteous moan that Rutland made

· · · · · · · · · · · · · · ·

                   —in that sad time
My manly eyes did scorn an humble tear;
And what these sorrows could not thence exhale,
Thy beauty hath, and made them blind with weeping.

                                (1.2.149–66)

The love-dazzled eyes in Richard's mirror are a monstrous parody, but the brilliance of the reflection blinds Anne's moral vision; and what it reveals to her is a kind of truth. These lovers' eyes get no babies, but they get, in different ways, themselves. In the moment of triumph Richard repeats his offer to kill himself in lines which mimic the mirror-ironies of divine justice:

    This hand, which for thy love did kill thy love,
    Shall for thy love kill a far truer love.

                          (1.2.189–90)

V

Richard III, as critics from Moulton to Tillyard have observed, continues the ironical pattern of nemesis established in the three plays which precede it: punishment follows crime in apparently endless sequence, as though Justice held a mirror to every act. But in this play there is an increasing tendency for the ironies to become self-reflexive: the biter bit becomes the biter bitten by himself. Buckingham's death speech reechoes the familiar "measure for measure" theme—"Wrong hath but wrong, and blame the due of blame" (5.1.29)—but recognizes a special malicious wit in the means:

    Why then All-Souls' day is my body's doomsday.
    · · · · · · · · · · · · · · ·
    This is the day wherein I wish'd to fall
    By the false faith of him whom most I trusted;

    · · · · · · · · · · · · · · ·

> That high All-Seer, which I dallied with,
> Hath turn'd my feigned prayer on my head,
> And given in earnest what I begg'd in jest.
> Thus doth he force the swords of wicked men
> To turn their own points in their masters' bosoms.
>
> (5.1.12–24)

There is an obviously ironical echo here of Richard's mock offer to Anne; and indeed God's modus operandi seems all too close to Richard's own. As Richard made Clarence's death a new baptism, so God makes All Souls' Day Doomsday for Buckingham. As Richard's mirrors turned Anne's and Margaret's curses, so God turns Buckingham's prayer back upon himself. (The mysterious episode of Hastings's encounter with the pursuivant in 3.2 is symbolically suggestive. The pursuivant, "also named Hastings," is a kind of mirror figure; and the meeting itself ironically mirrors the occasion of Hastings's previous visit to the Tower. The suggestion of unwitting self-division is appropriate; Hastings is putting his own head in the noose. The irony is complicated by the déjà vu, as though God were playing tricks with time.)

Richmond's concluding speech (which by its self-conscious appeal to the loyalties of the audience becomes a kind of epilogue, corresponding to Richard's "prologue") expresses the theme of self-division in political terms:

> England hath long been mad and scarr'd herself:
> The brother blindly shed the brother's blood,
> The father rashly slaughtered his own son,
> The son, compell'd, been butcher to the sire.
> All this divided York and Lancaster,
> Divided in their dire division.
>
> (5.5.23–28)

The events of the fifteenth century are seen as a history of progressive self-division—in the body politic; in its model, the family; and at last within the individual members of the physical body. Thus the motif of the divided self in *Richard III* is in a sense only the ultimate extension of the political argument. But what makes this a richer play than its predecessors is its new psychological focus. In the Duchess of York's lament in act 2, it is as though civil dissension were now reduced to a mere mirror of the inner crisis of the psychomachia:

> themselves, the conquerors,
> Make war upon themselves, brother to brother,
> Blood to blood, self against self.
>
> (2.4.61–63)

England, "this sickly land," as the citizens call it in 2.3, is infected by Edward's fatal sickness, a sickness which Richard mockingly describes as self-consumption:

> Now by Saint John, that news is bad indeed!
> O, he hath kept an evil diet long,
> And overmuch consum'd his royal person.
>
> (1.1.138–40)

Edward destroys himself as surely as the courtiers who gather about his deathbed in 2.1 and call down vengeance with their false oaths of friendship. And Margaret's warning to Elizabeth amid the bitter feuds of 1.3 has a general application: "Fool, fool! Thou whet'st a knife to kill thyself" (1.3.243). It is a warning which Elizabeth may recall in her final encounter with Richard in the second wooing scene:

> QUEEN ELIZABETH: Shall I forget myself to be myself?
> KING RICHARD: Ay, if yourself's remembrance wrong yourself.
>
> (4.4.420–21)

As the play develops, we are presented with the reality of the self-division that Elizabeth is talking about. Self-forgetfulness, the suppression of the moral self, leads at last to self-abandonment, to despair, as character after character is confronted by the consequences of his abdication:

> QUEEN ELIZABETH: Ah, who shall hinder me to wail and weep,
> To chide my fortune, and torment myself?
> I'll join with black despair against my soul,
> And to myself become an enemy.
>
> (2.2.34–37)

> ANNE: Lo, ere I can repeat this curse again,
> Within so small a time, my woman's heart
> Grossly grew captive to his honey words,
> And prov'd the subject of my own soul's curse.
>
> (4.1.77–80)

> BUCKINGHAM: That high All-Seer, which I dallied with,
> Hath turn'd my feigned prayer on my head,
> And given in earnest what I begg'd in jest.
>
> (5.1.20–22)

But the most potent version of the motif is once again in the scene of Clarence's murder. The politic self-division of Brakenbury, the pathetic moral stratagem of the murderers, the dramatized contest by which they attempt to objectify conscience as something outside themselves, all help to realize the process of self-division which has led to Clarence's condition of despair:

> Ah, Keeper, Keeper, I have done these things
> (That now give evidence against my soul).
>
> (1.4.66–67)

The first murderer's "Come, you deceive yourself" (1.4.245) reminds us that Clarence before, like the murderers now ("to their own souls blind," l. 255) has denied a part of himself. Such a denial is a kind of self-murder, and the drowning in Clarence's dream becomes a vivid metaphor for the suffocation of the moral self:

> and often did I strive
> To yield the ghost; but still the envious flood
> Stopp'd in my soul, and would not let it forth
> To find the empty, vast, and wand'ring air,
> But smother'd it within my panting bulk,
> Who almost burst to belch it in the sea.
>
> (1.4.36–41)

The imagery recalls Richard's self-torment in *3 Henry VI*:

> And I—like one lost in a thorny wood,
> That rents the thorns, and is rent with the thorns,
> Seeking a way, and straying from the way,
> Not knowing how to find the open air,
> But toiling desperately to find it out—
> Torment myself to catch the English crown.
>
> (*3 Henry VI*, 3.2.174–79)

Clarence's dream-death, however, proves to be a moral rebirth, just as the dream itself, like Richard's later, is a moral awakening: he dies, not to find the "empty air" of annihilation, but to be confronted by the ghosts of

Warwick and Prince Edward—as much the shadows of his murdered conscience as the shades of his murdered enemies.

If Clarence's dream becomes the chief imaginative symbol for the agonies of the divided self, it is in the character of Richard that the process of division is most fully embodied. Richard's perverted self-obsession—at once self-love and self-loathing—leads him to create a whole theater of false selves to conceal his true self from himself, a glass to contemplate his physical deformity in order to forget his inner formlessness. Ficino's *Commentary* again appears to throw some light upon the nature of this split. Ficino is seeking to explain Aristophanes' myth of the cloven man as a version of the Fall:

> "Men" (that is, the souls of men) "originally" (that is, when they were created by God), "were whole" and equipped with two lights, one natural, the other supernatural. . . . "They aspired to equal God"; they reverted to the natural light alone. Hereupon "they were divided," and lost their supernatural light, were reduced to the natural light alone, and fell immediately into bodies. "If they become too proud, they will again be divided"; that is, if they trust too much to natural ability, that innate and natural light which remains to them will also be extinguished in some way.
>
> (4.2)

> What has been debased is called, and correctly so, broken and "split" ["fractum . . . scissumque"].
>
> (4.5)

Richard's proclamation of his self-sufficiency ("I am myself alone") is nothing if not a revelation of the pride against which Ficino warns—"God alone, in whom nothing is lacking, above whom there is nothing, remains satisfied in himself and sufficient in himself, and therefore the soul made itself the equal of God, when it wished to be content with itself alone." (4.4)—and its consequence is the extinction of the natural light of conscience. Perhaps the cruelest of the many ironies at Richard's expense is that the very acts by which he attempts to assert his moral self-sufficiency are those which in fact declare his moral annihilation.

With Anne, Richard can make a game of the sort of self-division by which the murderers seek to excuse themselves (1.2.89–98) and a game of the final self-division of despair ("By such despair I should accuse myself," l. 85); and he can shrug off her attempts to remind him of the consistent relation of the self and its actions (ll. 99, 120). His insouciance is possible because, for Richard, the "self" has no moral continuity but is wholly defined in and by the immediate act, or performance—it is a projection, an image, a shadow in a glass. As there is no stable self to which responsibility can be referred, the deed can be acknowledged or denied as the dynamics of performance dictate: "Say that I slew them not?" (1.2.89). The last theatrical offer—"Then bid me kill myself, and I will do it." (1.2.186)—is in a sense perfectly genuine: for there is no self to kill, except a part. In his closing soliloquy, as he contemplates the imaginary mirror, Richard presents an almost infinitely refracted image of himself, as though reflected in the facets of a prism:

> *I* do not mistake *my person* all this while!
> Upon *my life*, she finds (although *I* cannot)
> *Myself* to be *a marv'llous proper man*.
> *I*'ll be at charges for a looking-glass,
> And entertain a score or two of tailors
> To study fashions to adorn *my body*:
> Since *I* am crept in favor with *myself*,
> *I* will maintain it with some little cost.
> But first *I*'ll turn yon fellow in his grave,
> And then return lamenting to *my* love.
> Shine out, fair sun, till *I* have bought a glass,
> That *I* may see *my shadow* as *I* pass.
>
> (1.2.252–63; italics mine)

The vertiginous *trompe l'oeil* multiplication of himself is meant as nothing more than a last exuberant display of his rhetorical sprezzatura, but it anticipates, with ironical precision, the appalling mirror-maze of his agony before Bosworth.

In act 1, scene 3, Richard again mocks the notion of self-enmity in his prayer for the pardon of Clarence's enemies:

> So do I ever—(*speaks to himself*) being well advis'd;
> For had I curs'd now, I had curs'd myself.
>
> (1.3.317–18)

Of course there is a sense in which Richard is already quite self-consciously his own enemy, as the following soliloquy suggests: "I do the wrong, and first begin to brawl" (1.3.323). The extent of his control over the action means that the other characters appear increasingly as pawns in an elaborate game played with himself. Making it his heaven to *dream upon* the crown rather than to actually possess it, Richard, like his kinsman Volpone, takes more pleasure in the cunning purchase than in the glad possession. Even Buckingham emerges as a kind of extension of Richard (Buckingham's argument on sanctuary [3.1.44ff.], for instance, precisely echoes the sophistry of Richard's advice to York regarding his oath to King Henry (3 Henry VI, 1.2.18–27); he speaks, in effect, with Richard's voice), "my other self" as Richard calls him (2.2.151). But Buckingham, too, conforms to the logic of the split self, and he turns against the king precisely at the point when Richard's own disintegration begins. The board at last swept clean of pieces, the player is left confronting . . . himself, the image in the glass.

Already in the first scene of act 4, Anne has given hints of shadows not in the sun:

> For never yet one hour in his bed
> Did I enjoy the golden dew of sleep,
> But with his timorous dreams was still awak'd.
> (4.1.82–84)

And in the following scene we become aware of the first conscious stirrings of Richard's suppressed moral self:

> But I am in
> So far in blood that sin will pluck on sin.
> (4.2.63–64)

It is as if the grotesque incest in butchery catalogued by Margaret in 4.4 has been pursued to the point where Richard himself is its only remaining object, the last of the issue of his mother's body on which the carnal cur may prey (4.4.56–57). His self, in Elizabeth's sarcastic retort (4.4.374) is "self-misus'd"; and when Richard picks up her gibe with a repetition of the self-cursing motif, there is behind the willed mockery an hysterical seriousness:

> Myself myself confound!
> Heaven and fortune bar me happy hours!
> Day, yield me not thy light, nor, night, thy rest!
> (4.4.399–401)

The confusion of the episode with Ratcliffe and Catesby, where for the first time the comedy is turned against Richard himself, immediately confirms the descent into psychological chaos, "the blind cave of eternal night."

Act 5, scene 3 is the last and physically most obvious of the play's mirror-scenes (recalling in its diagrammatic precision act 2, scene 5 of *3 Henry VI*, the episode of the son-who-has-killed-his-father and the father-who-has-killed-his-son). Now, however, the careful parallels in action and staging serve only to show how much the world is no longer Richard's mirror. The sun, which Richard greeted in the opening lines of the play and in which his shadow has sported for so long, makes its symbolic setting, and for Richard, at least, it is not to rise again. The last scene of his life is played in shadow.

In itself, as many critics have felt, the dream sequence is less than fully satisfying: it is probably the one point in the play where the mirror motif becomes obtrusively clumsy. The sequence is constructed as a kind of didactic mirror for magistrates, in which the false king is presented as the distorted mirror-image of the true. But at the same time it has to serve as an image of Richard's psychological torment, and the two functions are incompatible. As long as the ghosts are in Richard's dream, we can take them (like those in Clarence's dream) as shadows of his murdered conscience. The awkwardness arises when they appear in Richmond's, where, if they are not to appear as projections of a smug self-righteousness, they have to be taken as literal specters. The most telling part of the scene, however, is not the dream itself but the agony which follows it, in a speech which is at once the culmination and the fullest expression of the theme of the divided self.

Richard wakes in a sweat of terror from a dream prefiguring (shadowing) his death—"Give me another horse! Bind up my wounds!" (5.3.177)—and the terror gives a voice to self heard nowhere else in the play: "Have mercy, Jesu!" (l. 178). That cry in the dark has a poignancy absent from the conventional pieties of any of the apparently more virtuous characters. The voice, however unfamiliar, is one which Richard, like the murderers before him, recognizes well enough: "O coward conscience, how thou dost afflict me!" (l. 179) "Conscience" here has the full sense of "consciousness" as well as "moral awareness" and implies a total suppression of the inner life and hence of any true self:

> What do I fear? Myself? There's none else by.
> Richard loves Richard, that is, I [am] I.
>
> (5.3.182–83)

We are back here in the mirror world of the soliloquy at the end of 1.2. The reassertion of the old blasphemy, "I am I," is a despairing attempt to proclaim his self-sufficient integrity: "Richard loves Richard," the name is one with the namer; the image in the mirror is one with the self that sees it.

> Is there a murtherer here? No. Yes, I am.
> Then fly. What, from myself? Great reason why—
> Lest I revenge. What, myself upon myself?
> Alack, I love myself.
>
> (5.3.184–87)

But the struggle to remake the emblem of self-love (the looking glass of 1.2) inevitably collapses because Richard, the chameleon actor who has created himself only in his fleeting changes, can locate no stable self to love, no self solid enough to be loved:

> Alack, I love myself. Wherefore? For any good
> That I myself have done unto myself?
> O no! Alas, I rather hate myself
> For hateful deeds committed by myself.
>
> (5.3.187–90)

Indeed it proves impossible to find a locus for his self-loathing:

> I am a villain; yet I lie, I am not.
> Fool, of thyself speak well; fool, do not flatter.
>
> (5.3.191–92)

The self disintegrates into a babel of self-conflicting voices:

> My conscience hath a thousand several tongues,
> And every tongue brings in a several tale,
> And every tale condemns me for a villain.
>
> (5.3.193–95)

The cracked mirror becomes a fragmenting prism. And for a self so lost the only outlet is despair, because no single, integrated focus of consciousness exists, the only sound, the baying of a thousand several tongues:

> I shall despair; there is no creature loves me,
> And if I die no soul will pity me.
> Nay, wherefore should they, since that I myself
> Find in myself no pity to myself?
>
> (5.3.200–204)

Richard, who from the beginning has denied his kinship to the rest of humanity ("I am like no brother"), has thereby alienated himself from his own humanity: he is not like himself and therefore cannot love himself.

"A dream itself is but a shadow," and Richard's is a dream of shadows, refracted images of his own self, seen not by the artificial sun of his parody of godhead ("Shine out, fair sun") but looming in the blind cave of night:

> RATCLIFFE: Nay, good my lord, be not afraid of shadows.
> KING RICHARD: By the apostle Paul, shadows to-night
> Have strook more terror to the soul of Richard
> Than can the substance of ten thousand soldiers.
>   (5.3.215–18)

It is the last trick of God's dissembling mirror that Richard, who makes himself in shadows, is destroyed by shadows:

> I think there be six Richmonds in the field;
> Five have I slain to-day instead of him.
>   (5.4.11–12)

The best that Richard can manage in his last performance is a reincarnation of himself in the act. But while, even now, the energy is all his—"Come, bustle, bustle! Caparison my horse!" (5.3.289)—Richard is far from being (as Olivier gleefully announced) "himself again!" In the willful denial of conscience at the beginning of his oration to his army there must be a self-contradiction:

> Let not our babbling dreams afright our souls;
> Conscience is but a word that cowards use,
> Devis'd at first to keep the strong in awe:
> Our strong arms be our conscience, swords our law!
>   (5.3.308–11)

In the bravado of "A thousand hearts are great within my bosom" (l. 347), we can hardly fail to hear an echo of the babbling of conscience in its "thousand several tongues."

Act 5, scene 3 has been regarded, somewhat slightingly, as a theatrical tour de force. Of course, if one sets it beside the dramatizations of conscience in *Hamlet* or even *Macbeth*, it is certainly that. But what is so impressive is the sure dramatic instinct by which Shakespeare makes the limitations of his immature style work for him. The theatricality of Richard's conscience soliloquy becomes a positive strength because it corresponds so exactly to his own limitations. Where the inner self has been so systematically oppressed, there is no possibility of complex introspection. Richard's interior is a kingdom of night, a blind cave of shadows, at best a hall of mirrors, reflecting endlessly the insubstantial shadows of the lost self: a self he vainly tries to capture with the hopelessly inadequate tools of his old word-games. The cunning vice, Iniquity, moralizing two meanings in one word, is lost in the labyrinth of his own puns.

VI

If the conclusion of *Richard III* has a weakness, it is not in the dramaturgy of Richard's moral collapse but in the dramatist's moralization of his fall, in his refusal to confront the real issues which the play raises—though the refusal is, I suppose, inevitable. The ironies of the end are God's, and in their light the whole plot with its complex of witty peripeties is evidently the masterwork of a Cosmic Ironist. This being so, one finds oneself asking, despite Richmond's complacent pieties, isn't God only a greater and more competent Richard, fulfilling his fantasies of omnipotence, a malign demiurge delighting in the monstrous shadow of his own ugliness and obliterating it when it attempts to walk alone? Richard tries to declare his independence of the Ironist's tragic farce, to assert himself by making the world in his own image, a mirror-play of his own chaotic deformity, a glass to hold his shadow as he passes. His greatest sin lies in his attempt to become equal to God: the disturbing trouble is that, morally speaking, he appears to succeed.

"Neither Mother, Wife, nor England's Queen": The Roles of Women in *Richard III*

Madonne M. Miner

> *Richard sufficiently dominates the play so that analyses of his personality virtually exhaust the play's possibilities.*
>
> Psychoanalysis and Shakespeare

Although Norman Holland speaks here primarily with reference to psychoanalytic interpretations of Shakespeare's *Richard III*, his comment actually serves as indication of the initial assumption behind almost all critical readings of the play; literary critics generally indulge in an a priori and unacknowledged Forsterian division of characters into round (Richard) and flat (everyone else), focus upon the former, and then weave their own particular analytic threads according to patterns perceived in the character of Richard. Such threads comprise the traditional web of literary criticism—and deservedly so—but, because of the initial division of character and limitation of focus, certain questions raised by *Richard III* tend to fall outside the critical web. Why does one figure appear to assume a roundness of dimension while others, suffering from advanced anorexia, appear to atrophy? What is the nature of the interaction *among* "atrophied" figures as well as *between* such figures and the other, more "substantial" figure? This essay, organized into three sections, considers such questions with respect to one group of formerly ignored "flat characters": the women of *Richard III*. Section I studies the interaction between Richard and women, an inter-

From *The Woman's Part: Feminist Criticism of Shakespeare*, edited by Carolyn Ruth Swift Lenz, Gayle Greene, and Carol Thomas Neely. © 1980 by the Board of Trustees of the University of Illinois. University of Illinois Press, 1980.

action characterized by his determination to cast women in unattractive roles: as scapegoat for men, currency of exchange between men, and cipher without men. Section II suggests that interaction occurs among the women of the play, and Section III further substantiates the integrity of female figures with an analysis of the way in which metaphors of birth and pregnancy are used and abused throughout the play.

I

Richard III opens with a soliloquy, in which Richard, Duke of Gloucester, distinguishes time past, time present, and what he perceives to be time future:

> Grim-visaged War hath smoothed his wrinkled front,
> And now, instead of mounting barbed steeds
> To fright the souls of fearful adversaries,
> He capers nimbly in a lady's chamber
> To the lascivious pleasing of a lute.
> . . . .
> Why, I, in this weak piping time of peace,
> Have no delight to pass away the time.
> . . . .
> And therefore, since I cannot prove a lover
> To entertain these fair well-spoken days,
> I am determinèd to prove a villain.
>
> (1.1.9–13, 24–25, 28–30)

Out of step with his time, Richard determines to force it into closer conformity with his own nature. Implicitly, the quality of the present which Richard finds so onerous is its femininity; present days belong to "wanton ambling nymphs," not to marching warriors, not to hunchbacked younger brothers. The opposition between war and peace is expressed as opposition between male and female; "male" is associated with "bruisèd arms," "stern alarums," and "barbèd steeds," and "female" with "merry meetings," "delightful measures," and "sportive tricks." It makes no difference whether we agree or disagree with Richard's sexual collocations; what is of importance is Richard's exclusive identification with one side of the antithesis and his determination to obliterate those who represent the opposite—those who, according to the imagery of Richard's soliloquy, are women.

In addition to introducing the poles of opposition in *Richard III*,

Gloucester's opening soliloquy also introduces a tactic that Richard employs throughout: an allocation of guilt along sexual lines so that women are invariably at fault. Within the soliloquy it is apparent that women are to blame for effacing the countenance of "Grim-visaged War" and, immediately following the soliloquy, Richard explains to brother Clarence that women are to blame for other things as well. Even though Richard has just told us that he has spun "inductions dangerous" so as to set Clarence and Edward "in deadly hate the one against the other," when Clarence enters, under guard, Richard maintains that women are at the root of his woes:

> Why, this it is when men are ruled by women.
> 'Tis not the king that sends you to the Tower.
> My Lady Grey his wife, Clarence, 'tis she
> That tempers him to this extremity.
>
> (1.1.62–65)

Richard's allegation not only deflects suspicion from himself and onto Elizabeth, but also tends to unite the two brothers against an intruder (the sister-in-law, the "Other"). While challenging bonds of marriage, Richard appears to be reaffirming bonds of consanguinity. Clarence catches the impulse of Richard's comment and carries it yet further, naming Mistress Shore as another female force undermining the throne; if one woman is not to blame, another may be found. Clarence cites Shore's intervention in favor of Hastings and Richard agrees: "Humbly complaining to her deity / Got my Lord Chamberlain his liberty" (1.1.76–77). Obviously, according to Richard, when prostitutes capture the ear of kings, when wives wield more power than brothers, the time is out of joint.

In the subsequent exchange with Anne, who follows the corpse of her father-in-law Henry to Chertsey, as in that with Clarence, Richard directs culpability from himself and onto the female figure. He greets the recently widowed woman as "sweet saint" (1.2.49), and bolsters this greeting with a string of compliments, to which she responds with curses. When Anne charges him with the slaughter of her father-in-law, Henry VI, and her husband, Edward, Richard initially scrambles for a surrogate (blaming Edward IV and Margaret) but then hits upon a far more effective line, accusing Anne as the primary "causer" of the deaths:

> Your beauty was the cause of that effect;
> Your beauty, that did haunt me in my sleep

> To undertake the death of all the world,
> So I might live one hour in your sweet bosom.
>
> (1.2.121–24)

Thus, Anne is responsible; her beauty serves as incentive for murder. Richard, of course, lies; he kills Edward and Henry so as to come closer to the throne, and he woos Anne for the same reason. By the end of the scene, however, this hunchbacked Machiavellian is able to acknowledge his role in the murders of Edward and Henry, to offer Anne his sword to use against him, and to smile in the knowledge of his victory as she refuses to take vengeance.

> Nay, do not pause, for I did kill King Henry,
> But 'twas thy beauty that provokèd me.
> Nay, now dispatch; 'twas I that stabbed young Edward,
> But 'twas thy heavenly face that set me on.
> Take up the sword again, or take up me.
>
> (1.2.179–83)

By focusing on her beauty, Richard insists that Anne fit the very flat definition of "womankind" he articulated in his opening soliloquy—a definition that divides the world into male and female provinces, denying the latter any possibility of communion with emblems (such as swords) of the former. Focusing upon Anne's guilt, Richard deflects responsibility from himself, and constructs a bond of alliance between Anne and himself, against the House of Lancaster, rendering her powerless.

While the exchange between Richard and Anne may be the most dramatic example of Richard's aptitude with respect to sexual dynamics and the allocation of guilt, it is by no means a final example. Another variation occurs in act 3, scene 4, when Richard determines to weed out the ranks of those in opposition to his coronation. Because Hastings is involved with Mistress Shore, all Richard need do is accuse Shore, implicate Hastings (guilt by association) and be rid of him. Thus, in the midst of an assembly meeting, Richard draws forth his withered arm and announces: "And this is Edward's wife, that monstrous witch, / Consorted with that harlot strumpet Shore, / That by their witchcraft thus have markèd me" (3.4.69–71). Hastings's reply, "If they have done this deed, my noble lord" (l. 72), is twisted by an enraged Richard into unimpeachable evidence of guilt: "If! Thou protector of this damnèd strumpet, / Talk'st thou to me of ifs? Thou art a traitor. / Off with his head!" (ll. 73–75). In spite of the incredible and illogical nature of Richard's accusation (his arm has always been withered;

the association of Elizabeth and Mistress Shore as conspirators is extremely unlikely), it holds: Hastings loses his head on the basis of his involvement with a woman. Although the dynamics in the three examples cited above vary considerably, in each instance Richard blames women in order to benefit himself and, in so doing, he creates or destroys associational bonds between men.

If, in the scenes above, Richard is able to manipulate women and blame so as to cut or spin associational threads, his tailoring skills appear yet more impressive when he sets himself to matchmaking—an activity which appears to encourage the reduction of female status from "person" to "thing exchanged." As Lévi-Strauss observes in *Structural Anthropology*, marriage functions as the lowest common denominator of society; based as it has been on the exchange of a woman between two men, marriage brings together two formerly independent groups of men into a kinship system. Richard takes advantage of these associational possibilities, but, interestingly enough, the impulse behind his marital connections most often appears to be one of destruction rather than creation; society is wrenched apart rather than drawn together. We see Richard play the role of suitor twice, with Lady Anne and with Queen Elizabeth (whom he approaches to request the hand of her daughter Elizabeth). To be sure, in formulating his marital plans, Richard approaches women—an eligible widow and a widowed mother—but in both cases, Richard actually focuses on men behind the women. Before meeting Anne en route to Chertsey, he reveals his designs on her:

> For then I'll marry Warwick's youngest daughter.
> What though I killed her husband and her
>   father?
> The readiest way to make the wench amends
> Is to become her husband and her father.
>
> (1.1.153–56)

"To make the wench amends"? Such, of course, is not the actual motivation behind Richard's system of substitution; he realizes that in order to substantiate his claims to the position previously held by Henry VI, it is politic to align himself with Henry's daughter-in-law. Further, maneuvering himself into Anne's bedchamber, Richard moves closer to replacing Edward, former occupant thereof, and former heir to the throne. Thus, after killing Anne's "husband and father," Richard can assume their sexual and political roles. Finally, Richard's speech clarifies the function of women in the marital game: whether the game be one of exchange or one of substitution, the female serves as a piece to be moved *by others*, and a piece having value only *in relation* to others.

Political values, however, like those of the stock market, fluctuate wildly, and by act 4, Richard (now king) recognizes that Anne has out-lived her usefulness to him. After instructing Catesby to rumor it abroad that Anne is "very grievous sick," Richard ruminates alone: "I must be married to my brother's daughter, / Or else my kingdom stands on brittle glass. / Murder her brothers and then marry her!" (4.2.58–60). As in his earlier choice of bride, Richard here pursues a woman from whom he has taken all male relatives; although not fully responsible for the death of Elizabeth's father, Richard conspires to lessen the natural term of Edward's life, and he employs more direct measures with respect to Clarence (Eliza-beth's uncle) and the two princes (Elizabeth's brothers). However, not all possible rivals have been obliterated: Richmond also seeks the hand of Ed-ward's daughter, and Richard's awareness of a living male rival sharpens his desire to legitimize his claim:

> Now, for I know the Britain Richmond aims
> At young Elizabeth, my brother's daughter,
> And by that knot looks proudly on the crown,
> To her go I, a jolly thriving wooer.
>
> (4.3.40–43)

Elizabeth, of course, has been a loose end; with the young princes dead ("cut off") she remains the only legitimate possibility of access to the throne. By tying his own knots, Richard plans to exclude Richmond from making any claims to the kingdom. In sum, Richard woos both Anne and Elizabeth because of the position they occupy with respect to men. How-ever, in proposing marriage (which might lead to a bonding of male to male through female), Richard does not seek a union *with* other men but rather *replaces* them by assuming their roles with respect to women.

In considerations of the way Richard employs women as scapegoats and currency, younger female figures have received most attention. How-ever, when we consider how Richard uses women as ciphers, three older women—Queen Elizabeth, Margaret, and the Duchess of York—step, re-luctantly, into the foreground. All of these women suffer, on one level, a loss of definition at the hand of Richard. Caught in a society that conceives of women strictly in relational terms (that is, as wives to husbands, moth-ers to children, queens to kings), the women are subject to loss of title, position, and identity, as Richard destroys those by whom women are de-fined: husbands, children, kings. Early in the play, Queen Elizabeth perceives the precarious nature of *her* position as her husband, King Edward, grows weaker and weaker. "The loss of such a lord includes all harms" (1.3.8), she tells her son Grey. Elizabeth's words find verification not only in later scenes, but also, here, before Edward's death, in the figure of Margaret, England's former queen. Margaret, hiding in the wings, listens as Richard taunts Elizabeth and accuses her of promoting her favorites. When Elizabeth replies, "Small joy have I in being England's Queen" (l. 109), Margaret can barely restrain herself; she says in an aside: "As little joy enjoys the queen thereof; / For I am she, and altogether joyless" (ll. 154–55). Margaret's aside pinpoints the confusion that results when women must depend upon men for identity and when Richard persists in removing these men. Is a woman to be considered "queen" after her "king" has been killed? Does one's title apply only as long as one's husband is alive? And, after her husband's death, what does the "queen" become? Margaret serves, of course, as model for the women of *Richard III*; she enters in act 1 and shows Elizabeth and the Duchess of York what they have to expect from the future; like her, they are destined to years of sterile widowhood. But the women of York do not yet perceive Margaret's function; with Richard, they mock her and force her from the stage. Before leaving, however, Margaret further clarifies her relationship to Elizabeth by underlining the similarity of their woes:

> Thyself a queen, for me that was a queen,
> Outlive thy glory like my wretched self!
> Long mayst thou live to wail thy children's death;
>
> . . . .
>
> Long die thy happy days before thy death,
> And, after many length'ned hours of grief,
> Die neither mother, wife, nor England's Queen!
> (1.3.201–3, 206–8)

Alive—but neither mother, wife, nor England's queen: the description may apply to Margaret, Elizabeth, and the Duchess. Only a very short time elapses between the day of Margaret's curse and the day Elizabeth suffers the death of her lord. Addressing the Duchess, the twice-widowed woman cries: "Edward, my lord, thy son, our king, is dead! / Why grow the branches when the root is gone? / Why wither not the leaves that want their sap?" (2.2.40–42). Elizabeth's questions forecast her upcoming tragedy.

Not only does Richard subvert the role of queen, he also undermines roles of mother and wife. For example, while the death of Edward robs

Elizabeth of a husband, it robs the Duchess of York of a son. Having lost
son Clarence earlier, the Duchess's "stock" suffers a depletion of two-
thirds. She turns to Elizabeth, commenting that years ago she lost a worthy husband.

> And lived with looking on his images;
> But now two mirrors of his princely semblance
> Are cracked in pieces by malignant death,
> And I for comfort have but one false glass
> That grieves me when I see my shame in him.
> Thou art a widow, yet thou art a mother
> And hast the comfort of thy children left.
>
> (2.2.50–56)

Stressing Elizabeth's yet-current claim to motherhood, the Duchess appears to abjure her own; it is as if she no longer wants to assume the title
of mother if Richard is the son who grants her this right; accepting "motherhood" means accepting responsibility for "all these griefs," for the losses
sustained by Elizabeth and by Clarence's children.

It is not enough for one mother to abandon her claim to the title of
mother; Richard pursues a course of action that eventually forces Elizabeth
to relinquish her claim also (note that as the play proceeds, Elizabeth
comes to bear a closer resemblance to Margaret). The process leading to
Elizabeth's forfeiture of her title is more complicated than that of the
Duchess and is accomplished in a series of steps: Buckingham and Richard
override maternal authority and, parenthetically, the right of sanctuary, by
"plucking" the Duke of York from the sheltering arms of his mother; Brakenbury, under order from Richard, denies Elizabeth entrance to the
Tower, thereby denying her right to see her children; Richard casts doubt
on the legitimacy of Edward's marriage to Elizabeth, and hence, on the
legitimacy of her children; Richard preys upon Elizabeth to grant him her
daughter in marriage while Elizabeth knows that to do so would be to sentence her daughter to a living death.

As this process is set in motion, the "Protector" refuses to grant Elizabeth her status as mother; as it comes to a close, Elizabeth freely abjures
her motherhood in an attempt to protect her remaining child. Up until the
murder of her sons, Elizabeth insists, often futilely, upon her maternal
rights. When, for example, Brakenbury refuses to admit her to the Tower,
she protests violently upon the grounds of familial relation: "Hath he set
bounds between their love and me? / I am their mother; who shall bar me
from them?" (4.1.20–21). Almost as if she were determined actively to dis-

pute Richard's allegations that her children are illegitimate, Elizabeth reiterates, time and time again, the status of her relationship and that of her children to Edward. After the deaths of young Edward and Richard, however, Elizabeth is forced to perform an about-face. Because of Richard's manipulations, a "mother's name is ominous to children"; hence, she must deny her title of mother in order to express her genuine identity as a mother concerned for her children's welfare. She dispatches her son Dorset to France—"O Dorset, speak not to me, get thee gone!" (4.1.38)—and expresses her willingness to deny the legitimacy of young Elizabeth's birth to save her from marriage to Richard.

> And must she die for this? O, let her live,
> And I'll corrupt her manners, stain her beauty,
> Slander myself as false to Edward's bed,
> Throw over her the veil of infamy;
> So she may live unscarred of bleeding slaughter,
> I will confess she was not Edward's daughter.
>
> (4.4.206–11)

It is the love of a mother for her daughter which prompts Elizabeth's offer; she willingly renounces her titles both of wife and legitimate mother.

In the examples cited above, Richard's general course of action is such to encourage women to abandon traditional titles, to de-identify themselves. Richard more specifically encourages this cipherization by confounding the integrity of titular markers: that is, by juggling titles without regard for the human beings behind these titles (although Richard does not restrict himself to female markers, females suffer more grievously from these verbal acrobatics than do males, who may draw upon a wider range of options with respect to identifying roles). Richard's changing choice of title for his sister-in-law Elizabeth most clearly exemplifies his policy of confoundment. Richard's first reference to Elizabeth occurs in a conversation with Clarence, in which Richard promises that he will employ any means to procure his brother's freedom: "And whatsoe'er you will employ me in, / Were it to call King Edward's widow sister, / I will perform it to enfranchise you" (1.1.108–10). Several things are happening here. First, as the wife of Edward, Richard's brother, Elizabeth *is* Richard's sister (sister-in-law); she need not solicit the title from Richard, although Richard certainly implies that it is his prerogative to grant or withhold the title at will. Second, the title Richard actually bestows on Elizabeth is "King Edward's widow," an equivocation of marvelous subtlety; Elizabeth *is* the widow of Grey but Richard's phrasing makes it possible to read this description as a prediction: Elizabeth will wear weeds again. And finally, when Richard and Elizabeth meet in the following scene, it is Elizabeth who twice addresses Richard as "Brother Gloucester"; Richard refuses to call her anything, because, at this time, he has nothing to gain by doing so. Later, in act 2, following the convenient demise of Edward IV, Richard, as if to ensure a smooth transference of power, attempts to placate Elizabeth: he calls her "sister." In act 4, however, after Richard has approached Elizabeth for the hand of young Elizabeth, he calls her "mother": "Therefore, dear mother—I must call you so— / Be the attorney of my love to her" (4.4.412–13). The exchange between Richard and Elizabeth also supplies a rather startling example of Richard's indifference to the human beings who actually give substance to the titles he juggles with such apparent ease. Richard insists that he will provide substitutes for the children Elizabeth lost at his hand:

> To quicken your increase I will beget
> Mine issue of your blood upon your daughter.
> A grandam's name is little less in love
> Than is the doting title of a mother.
>
> (4.4.297–300)

Focusing exclusively upon a "grandam's *name*" and the "*title* of a mother," Richard attempts to obscure the very real difference between these two positions; he attempts to confound all meaning attached to female position markers—a policy in keeping with his determination to confound women altogether.

II

Given Richard's perception of woman as enemy, as "Other," we should not be surprised that the action of the play depends upon a systematic denial of the human identity of women. Richard's apparently successful attempts to obscure Elizabeth's titular "sense of self" and Elizabeth's rejection of both her own identity and that of her daughter exemplify, on one level, the progression of women in *Richard III*: from mother to nonmother, wife to widow, queen to crone. However, this "progression" does not take into account a less obvious and more positive progression of women from a condition of bickering rivalry to a condition of sympathetic camaraderie. In the midst of loss, the women turn to each other. Thus, an interesting, but generally ignored, countermotion of interaction *among* women is introduced; having been reduced to the condition of nothing,

Margaret, Elizabeth, and the Duchess evidence a new humanity, a humanity apparent nowhere else in the play. We need only explore the progression in the four scenes in *Richard III* in which women confront each other (1.3; 2.2; 4.1; 4.4) to see this countermotion. Act 1, scene 3, opens with Elizabeth and Richard at each other's throat; with the entrance of Margaret, however, Richard is able to direct all hostility toward her. Even Elizabeth joins with crook-backed Gloucester in condemning the widow of Lancaster; angry words fly across the stage. When Elizabeth applauds Richard for turning Margaret's curse back on herself, Margaret chides the "poor-painted queen":

> Why strew'st thou sugar on that bottled spider
> Whose deadly web ensnareth thee about?
> Fool, fool, thou whet'st a knife to kill thyself.
> The day will come that thou shalt wish for me
> To help thee curse this poisonous bunch-backed toad.
>
> (1.3.241–45)

Margaret's prediction proves true, but the women must suffer first.

If the preceding scene depicts the hostility between women of different houses, act 2, scene 2, depicts hostility between women of the same House. Instead of coming together in sympathy upon learning of the deaths of Clarence and Edward, the women of York and the children of Clarence engage in a chorus of moans, each claiming the greater loss. An appalling absence of empathy characterizes this meeting. A few lines may serve to indicate the mood of the entire scene:

> DUCHESS: O, what cause have I,
>   Thine being but a moi'ty of my moan,
>   To overgo thy woes and drown thy cries!
> BOY: Ah, aunt, you wept not for our father's death.
>   How can we aid you with our kindred tears?
> DAUGHTER: Our fatherless distress was left unmoaned;
>   Your widow-dolor likewise be unwept!
> ELIZABETH: Give me no help in lamentation;
>   I am not barren to bring forth complaints.
>
> (2.2.59–67)

Obviously, the tendency here is away from commiseration and toward a selfish indulgence. It is not until act 4, scene 1, that a reversal of this tendency begins to make itself felt, the result of the women's sympathy as their position continues to erode. Elizabeth, the Duchess of York, Anne, and Clarence's daughter meet en route to the Tower to greet the young princes. When Elizabeth is denied visitation privileges, the Duchess and Anne support her maternal rights. Even when Stanley announces that Anne is to be crowned queen, the bond of sympathy between Anne and Elizabeth is not destroyed. Given her history of suffering, Elizabeth can respond now with feeling to Anne as Margaret could not when she was replaced by Elizabeth. When the new queen expresses her wish that the "inclusive verge of golden metal" were "red-hot steel to sear me to the brains," Elizabeth attempts to console her: "Go, go, poor soul! I envy not thy glory. / To feed my humor wish thyself no harm" (4.1.63–64). The Duchess of York adds her blessing also: "Go thou to Richard, and good angels tend thee!" (l. 92). How different from the feeling of act 2, scene 2! Even though this union of sympathy may not generate any practical power (Richard continues to confound the women) it does prompt a revision in our responses to them: they attain a tragic dignity.

The most moving example of women-aiding-women, however, occurs in act 4, scene 4, where the women of York join Margaret of Lancaster in cursing Richard. This union is achieved only gradually. Old Queen Margaret enters alone and withdraws to eavesdrop on Elizabeth and the Duchess of York, who sit down together to lament the death of the princes and lament their uselessness: "Ah that thou wouldst as soon afford a grave / As thou canst yield a melancholy seat" (4.4.31–32). When Margaret comes forward and joins the two women on the ground, she first claims that her griefs "frown on the upper hand" and it seems the scene will be a reiteration of the earlier contest.

> If sorrow can admit society,
> Tell o'er your woes again by viewing mine.
> I had an Edward, till a Richard killed him;
> I had a husband, till a Richard killed him.
> Thou hadst an Edward, till a Richard killed him.
> Thou hadst a Richard, till a Richard killed him.
>
> (4.4.38–43)

The Duchess, catching the rhythm of Margaret's refrain, interrupts in order to wail a few lines of her own. Margaret, however, regains voice, reminding the Duchess that it is her womb that has bred the cause of all their sorrows: "From forth the kennel of thy womb hath crept / A hellhound that doth hunt us all to death" (4.4.47–48). These words signal a reversal in the dynamics of the scene; no longer willing to recognize the legal ties to men which prohibit a communion between women of different parties, these women join together in sorrow, in suffering; it is easy enough to imagine the three of them, seated on the earth, hand in hand. The Duchess abandons her competition with Margaret for the title of most grief-stricken, and turns, in commiseration, to her: "O Harry's wife, triumph not in my woes! / God witness with me I have wept for thine"(ll. 59–60). Elizabeth, too, moves toward Margaret, admitting that the prophesied time has come for her to request Margaret's help in cursing the "foul bunch-backed toad" (l. 81) Richard. Thus, the exchange among the women leads to the decision to arm themselves (to assume a male prerogative) with words; Margaret provides lessons in cursing and the Duchess suggests that they smother Richard in "the breath of bitter words" (l. 133); no more wasted or feeble words—instead, the women now use words as weapons. Accordingly, when Richard enters a short while after Margaret's departure, Elizabeth and the Duchess verbally accost and accuse him. Unaccustomed to such noise, an indignant Richard commands: "Either be patient and entreat me fair, / Or with the clamorous report of war / Thus will I drown your exclamations" (ll. 152–54). Richard's response to these insistent female voices is worthy of note as it reiterates the alliance of Richard with war and against women, and as it serves as summary statement of Richard's policy with respect to women—they must be silenced. The Duchess, however, finds voice, and her final words to Richard take the form of a curse; she turns against her own house, prays for the adverse party, and damns her son Richard to a death of shame. Her ability to do so with such strength is surely a result of the communion of sympathy shared by the three women. If, in previous scenes, a meeting of women merely leads to angry words and altercation, the meeting of act 4, scene 4, leads to the formation of bonds among the women against a single foe. When the progression of female characters is charted on this level, it becomes apparent that they do not deserve the a priori dismissal they too frequently receive. Although attenuated by Richard, women take on an emotional solidity, a roundness of true humanity.

III

A consideration of birth metaphor clarifies, yet further, the paradoxically double presentation of women in *Richard III*; specifically, perversion of birth metaphors suggests the negative condition of women articulated in section 1 (from mother to nonmother, etc.), while the persistence and importance of these metaphors suggest the very positive condition of women articulated in section 2 (as individuals having considerable power and human value). Although examples of the birth metaphor are so numerous as to render selection a problem, three categories may be arbitrarily distinguished: metaphor as descriptive of the condition of the times; as descriptive of Richard's activities and of Richard himself from the perspective of other characters; and as descriptive of Richard's mind as revealed in his own comments.

As mentioned previously, Richard "declares war" on the present time in his opening soliloquy; the extent to which he realizes this declaration may be felt in comments made by other characters throughout the play about the changed condition of the times—comments which most often work through a distortion of imagery usually associated with birth. When a group of citizens gathers to discuss the recent death of Edward and the probable confusion that will result, one compares his apprehension of ensuing danger to the swelling of water before a boisterous storm (2.3.42–45). Although "swelling" is not, by any means, a term associated exclusively with pregnancy, it almost always conveys a feeling of pregnant expectation. Here, and at all other times throughout *Richard III*, that which is expected, that which swells the body, is something ominous, something negative. This consistently pejorative use of the term "swelling" stands in contrast to a possible positive application of the word: that is, swelling as indicative of a generous fertility. A similarly pejorative application of usually positive terms occurs in the speech of Elizabeth when she, like the citizens, is informed of Edward's death. Refusing all offers of sympathy from others, she cries: "I am not barren to bring forth complaints. / All springs reduce their currents to mine eyes, / That I . . . / May send forth plenteous tears to drown the world" (2.2.67–68, 70). Two aspects of Elizabeth's choice of metaphor are worthy of note. First, the widow asserts her fertility, but a fertility that gives birth to complaints, instead of children. Second, the "children" that Elizabeth does produce assume the shape of tears, tears which, under normal conditions, might function as springs of life. Given the corruption of conditions under Richard, however, Elizabeth sends forth her tears to destroy life, "to drown the world."

Examination of Richard's specific activities reveals more explicitly his perversion of regenerative processes. When the thugs employed to murder Clarence attempt to convince him that Richard is the father of this deed, Clarence shakes his head in disbelief: "It cannot be, for he bewept my fortune / And hugged me in his arms and swore with sobs / That he would labor my delivery" (1.4.247–49). While Clarence assumes that Richard will "deliver" him from prison, to freedom, Richard intends to deliver Clarence from prison to death. Thus, Richard reverses the normal delivery process; instead of drawing Clarence forth from the womb, two midwives push him back into a yet darker womb (specifically, into a butt of malmsey). The speech of Tyrrel, another murderer employed by Richard, provides a second commentary on Richard's activities. Having commissioned the execution of the young princes, he tells the king: "If to have done the thing you gave in charge / Beget your happiness, be happy then, / For it is done" (4.3.25–27). "The thing" given in charge is the murder of two children; once more, begetting and killing are conjoined. The comments of Margaret and the Duchess affirm this unnatural conjunction, transferring it to the literal level: Richard's unnatural birth. Margaret attacks Richard as "Thou slander of thy heavy mother's womb! / Thou loathèd issue of thy father's loins!" (1.3.230–31). Similarly, because of son Richard, the Duchess of York cries out against her own womb, revealing an extreme of female debasement and acceptance of guilt: "O my accursèd womb, the bed of death! / A cockatrice hast thou hatched to the world, / Whose unavoided eye is murderous" (4.1.53–55). Richard, forcing an association of the womb with "the bed of death," succeeds, at least *partially*, in debasing the value of women, these creatures with wombs.

One final category of defective birth imagery is that employed by Richard in describing his own activities. After the general altercation of act 1, scene 3, for example, Richard steps off alone and comments: "I do the wrong, and first begin to brawl. / The secret mischiefs that I *set abroach* / I lay unto the grievous charge of others" (1.3.323–25, emphasis added). Or, just a short time later, when Edward, unaware of Richard's expeditious execution of Clarence, informs his court that peace has been made "between these swelling wrong-incensèd peers," Richard replies: "A blessèd *labor* my most sovereign lord" (2.1.52–53, emphasis added). But undoubtedly the most graphic of the many examples of debasement of the language of birth occurs in act 4, scene 4, as Richard encourages Elizabeth to allow him to right previous wrongs by marrying her daughter. When Elizabeth protests, "Yet thou didst kill my children," Richard counters: "But in your daughter's womb I'll bury them, / Where in that nest of spicery they will breed / Selves of themselves, to your recomforture" (4.4.423–25). Richard will bury old Elizabeth's children in young Elizabeth's womb? Could Richard hit upon a line of argument any more perversely unnatural? Up to this point, most birth metaphors have been constructed so as to suggest that the womb breeds no good (as, for example, that the Duchess's womb breeds a cockatrice); here, Richard forces the metaphor to work in reverse as well: the womb serves as tomb, functioning as both sprouting ground and burial plot. In forcing this perverse alliance of terms, Richard reaffirms, on a linguistic level, the impulse behind all of his activities with respect to women—the impulse to silence, to negate. Yet, paradoxically, the persistence with which Richard acts upon this impulse gives the lie to the possibility of its fulfillment: Richard's *need* to debase birth imagery implies that women (those capable of giving birth) have a power which finally cannot be devalued or eliminated; further, his repeated attempts, on a larger level, to rob women of their identity as mothers, wives, or queens, are doomed to frustration in that he cannot rob women of their identity as creative, regenerative human beings.

Richard III opens with a series of complaints directed, implicitly, against women. It is women who tame "Grim-visaged War," who caper to lutes, who play Love's games—and who govern the times. *Richard III* ends with a series of scenes on the battlefield; men engage in combat with men, and women are nowhere to be found (the last female on stage appears in act 4). On one level, the process of the play is one of denial and deflation; as Richard destroys husbands, kings, and children, as he confounds traditionally stable sources of identity and subjects women to an unnatural association with the forces of death, he suggests that women are without value—or, even worse, that they are destructive of value. But a reading of *Richard III* on just this one level does an injustice to the play; running parallel to the process described above is a counterprocess, one that insists upon the inherently positive value of women. We see evidence of this counterprocess in the progression of women from a condition of rivalry, battling amongst themselves, to a condition of camaraderie, sympathizing with each other, and in the persistence of the attack that Richard feels compelled to wage, both in life and in language, against these powerful foes. Even Richmond's final speech contributes to our sense of the invincibility of these females; after describing the bloody hatred between brothers which has divided England, Richmond proposes a reunification through his conjunction with the young woman Elizabeth. Hence, the argument of *Richard III* moves in two directions. The first insists that women are purely media of exchange and have no value in themselves; the second, overriding the first, insists that even when used as currency, women's value cannot be completely destroyed.

The Dead-End Comedy of *Richard III*

John W. Blanpied

Richard is a great role, as Richard himself was the first to discover in his coming-out soliloquy in *3 Henry VI*. All his predecessors—in Shakespeare, Marlowe, More, and elsewhere—are superseded by the way theatricality is built into his character. He is "sent" into the "world," incomplete: he is not of it, has no fixed identity, no "character" but the unique freedom of the self-creating actor. It is painful—he can see that the world that rejects him is not worth having, that worldly power is a sham and worldly attachments worse than nothing—but it is also exhilarating because he alone stands undetermined by that world's laws and rhythms. In fact, he can create himself by mocking down the world. That will be his plot, the action through which he will become a character. He is not born into this plot, this role; he creates them. He creates "history" by showing how lifeless and manipulable, how insubstantial it is in the hands of a mocking artist.

His first soliloquy in *3 Henry VI* is the locus classicus of machiavellian theatrics: energetic performing power, the proliferation of selves through dissembling roles, in the service of an ultimate goal, the crown. But the machiavel itself is a role in *Richard III*. It is played by Buckingham, Richard's "other self," who has mastered the "deep tragedian's" arsenal of effects as a means toward the end of worldly power. In his opening monologue Richard himself does not allude to the crown; he mentions it only glancingly after meeting Clarence, and not at all in his exuberance

From *Time and the Artist in Shakespeare's English Histories*. © 1983 by Associated University Presses, Inc.

after seducing Anne. For two acts he scarcely considers the ends of acting. Foremost in the dramatic persona comes the self-delighting antic, for whom the world is so corrupt and stupid that the satisfactions to be gained in mocking it cannot compare with those of regarding himself, his own audience, in a glass, and descanting on his own deformity. With Buckingham, then, he begins to play for power; but even then we watch the antic playing the machiavel:

> My other self, my counsel's consistory,
> My oracle, my prophet, my dear cousin,
> I, as a child, will go by thy direction.
>
> (2.2.151–53)

The self-delighting antic is invisible to Buckingham. In Richard he really sees himself.

The antic thrives on absolute antithesis. Richard would "undertake the death of all the world" (1.2.123), wants "the world for me to bustle in" (1.1.152), "all the world to nothing!" (1.2.237). It is idle to wag a finger at this anarchic individualism as if it were an embarrassment. It is his study, his pride, his art, to create himself in radical opposition to the world—meaning "history," the sum total of everyone else's experience; to perfect himself in opposition to everything that is not himself. Such rigorous economy surely masks a powerful fantasy, bound to be exposed sooner or later, but for awhile it pleases us to be engaged by Richard's sheer performing verve. And besides, coming fresh from the clamor of *Henry VI*, we must welcome a theatrical mode that presents such deftly vivid distinctions. Probably no play was ever before pitched to its audience with such subtly knowing calculation as is *Richard III* in its opening gesture. The cool precision of Richard's rhetorical stance disavows bombast, sentimentality, vagueness; it asserts dry clarity. It gives enough of a "character" to seem fascinating, not so much as to muddy our immediate perception, or disturb the grounds of our engagement. It offers, in other words, a uniquely theatrical gratification.

The opening is a masterful tease, a great theater game; the speech is a wonderful blend of self-disclosure and self-concealment, or so it seems. Richard is bored, an unemployed actor in "this weak piping time of peace"; therefore, since he cannot have war and cannot enjoy lust, "I am determinèd to prove a villain." This is a coldly aesthetic aim, and curiously abstract, as if the nature of the villainy were unimportant. Like Iago, that other trickster, he is something of a *bricoleur*, working from available materials: if they are rotten to begin with, what can he do? At least he will make the rottenness intelligible, answerable, by shaping it as his opposition, his Not-me. He does not say "I am a villain," but "I will try myself out in the role of 'villain.' " We respond first to the fiction of intimate disclosure, privileged confidence. We respond second to the thinly hidden "self," the perhaps tortured and suffering self, seeking compensatory gratification for psychic damage, or at least a kind of suffering we can only faintly perceive. Yet the tone is cool and elegant, the theater game superb, and safe. He "reveals" a dramatic persona exclusively to us, while being sure to suggest an underlying character only slightly deployed in this action, and not accountable to it. He implies in his performing verve that his energies derive from a source other than "history," "this breathing world." He is somehow autonomous, independent, unfathomable. Yet that hidden character may be a dramatic persona, too, glimpsed "behind" the first one. Our emerging doubts about the authenticity of a "self" within these roles constitutes a third line of awareness.

Tamburlaine is obviously Marlowe's darling, his speech strong because it is Marlowe's, and he consumes the world because it is so shadowy to begin with. But Richard is autonomous and self-creating (with a hint of something cogent underneath) and the world he encounters is highly organized and operates on iron and distinctive laws. Indeed, the antithesis between Richard and the "world" takes the overdetermined and fantastical form of two opposing modes of drama.

Richard's is obvious enough—a highly personal mode of aggressive mimicry, the assumption of others' voices, masks, stances, in order to mock them down. He specializes in parody—thrives on others' hypocrisy, pries open dissociations, exposes the passive will beneath aggressive language, leads his victims to the destruction, the punishment, the negation, they secretly desire. He perfects himself through furious activity, but success depends on his remaining, though Crookback and prominent, invisible. ("I would I knew thy heart," says Anne; " 'Tis figured in my tongue," he replies. Unlike Tamburlaine, his tongue is not gorgeous or Senecan, except in mockery. He is always ironic, his voice never his "own" except, perhaps, in soliloquy, though even this is a cool illusion.)

The world that Richard opposes is the radical reduction of historical experience in the *Henry VI* plays (where no such clearly defined world exists) into a Providential drama of the most static, mechanical, and impersonal kind:

> That high All-seer which I dallied with
> Hath turned my feignèd prayer on my head
> And given in earnest what I begged in jest.
>
> (5.1.20–22)

This is Buckingham, but it could be almost any of Richard's victims. Distinctions among them are tenuous, ghostly—feigned. What gives this world its peculiar unity, its definition as a play (that is, as shaped rather than "natural") is Margaret, who appears as its spokesman, and in a sense as Richard's rival dramatist. Not that she creates anything personally; her function is to reveal God's play, which she does through curses and prophecies. She appears only twice, the first time to announce the plot as a series of providential reprisals, the second to recapitulate and confirm the plot:

> Edward thy son, that now is Prince of Wales,
> For Edward our son, that was Prince of Wales,
> Die in his youth by like untimely violence!
>
> (1.3.198–200)

(Never mind that the violence is "like" only in being "untimely": her vision, like her speech, makes distinctions only between "mine" and "thine.")

> Thy Edward he is dead, that killed my Edward;
> Thy other Edward dead, to quit my Edward.
>
> (4.4.63–64)

"Here in these confines slily have I lurked," she intones, "witness" to the "dire induction" of events inexorably coming to pass. She uses the theatrical metaphor to suggest that a superior play has fulfilled itself through Richard, the scourge-of-God. What she "witnesses" is a parodic morality play in her own image: barren (gutted by a lifetime of brutality and suffering), external, mechanical, empty of personality and motivation, its single causative principle a reflex quid-pro-quo reaction, action itself conceivable only as crime, and the past (*Henry VI*) reduced to a series of crimes to be harvested in the present. The present is All Souls' Day, Judgment Day, the day when history itself is brought to an end. Margaret, in other words, "witnesses" a play about the end of playing.

What makes her so apt a rival to Richard is her very gratuitousness, her ghastly detachment, her disembodied instrumentality. Her entire character is emptied into her function as Prophet, and she is uniquely impotent as a character, incapable of acting (in either sense of the word), of withholding or deploying a "self" or of influencing any action. (All Richard's victims pay tribute to her power, but after the fact: they are all very eager to read their fates in her table of curses, to see the world in her quid-pro-quo terms. Clarence alone—whom she doesn't curse—experiences guilt and terror internally, rather than homiletically.) Margaret, in other words, is archetypal, Richard existential. She is (or has become) her function, bound to her language. But Richard, essenceless, has no language of his own, only parodies others', turning it back murderously upon them:

QUEEN MARGARET:
    [after sixteen lines of cursing]
        thou detested—
RICHARD:
      Margaret.
MARGARET:
        Richard!
RICHARD:
         Ha!
MARGARET:
           I call thee not.
RICHARD: I cry thee mercy then; for I did think
      That thou hadst called me all these bitter names.
MARGARET:Why, so I did, but looked for no reply.
      O, let me make the period to my curse!
RICHARD:'Tis done by me, and ends in "Margaret."
                              (1.3.232–38)

Margaret has, undeniably, a kind of brute theatrical force, though it derives from—it consummates—the tradition of declamatory assertiveness so prominent in the *Henry VI* plays, and which we discovered to be the manifestation of the self-paralyzing will that emerged as "history": the dissociation of men from their own experience. In its helplessness, its mindlessness, and its deep antipathy toward acting, Margaret's theater-mode radically opposes Richard's, but they are yoked together. Margaret's curses have a potential power to anyone secretly sharing her outright belief in magical language—which means everyone but Richard. Buckingham, the pragmatist, knows that "curses never pass / The lips of those that breathe them in the air" (1.3.284–85), and yet the future ghost, witness of the inexorable justice of the "high All-Seer," admits that "My hair doth stand on end to hear her curses" (l. 303). Richard, at this, makes a truly strange response: is it simply perverse (to keep Elizabeth and the others off balance) or is it perversely nonironic (thereby unbalancing us)? In either case, by voicing a humane sympathy for Margaret as crazed victim of the past rather than its prophet, he undercuts her authority:

    I cannot blame her. By God's holy
      Mother,

> She hath had too much wrong, and I
>   repent
> My part whereof that I have done to her.
>   (1.3.305–7)

Part of our pleasure comes from the obvious pretense that Richard is the underdog, triumphing against overwhelming odds, "all the world to nothing." He counts the obstacles between him and the crown. But they all come down quite readily, and, in fact, he never does seem to sweat until after he has the crown, never seems passionate or panicky in his operations. Not only is he not an underdog, but even the scrupulously overdetermined structure of antitheses, of matched opposites, is spurious: the manifestation of a fantasy of power. It is not just that his victims are willingly victimized, though that is true, but also that their willingness traps Richard into a reflexive role of easy mastery that gradually hardens into a kind of slavishness. In working the ironic fulfillment of the peers' dissembling vows—"So thrive I mine!" and so forth—Richard seems to fulfill his own role in Margaret's program as "hell's black intelligencer; / Only reserved their factor to buy souls / And send them thither" (4.4.71–73). It is precisely the pallid ease, however, with which these "souls" first dissemble and then, reflexively, suffer their reversals, that as characters makes them so shadowy, such parodic play figures, and hence such contemptible victims. Richard knows this—that is why the machiavel, who values the world he scorns, is a second-rate role. One may even imagine a Richard nauseated by his victims' compulsive will to be used, to be "shadows." Just this kind of puppetry provoked his dramatic insurgence in the first place (in *3 Henry VI*, 3.2), and now it appears that all his fiercely cool manipulating energy is bound to the ultimately futile activity of making shadows of shadows.

But the play's structure is so clear, so welcome, and so brilliantly exploited for three acts by Richard that it frees our responses for pleasure in his nimbleness, and we accede to fictions we would not find suspect anywhere but in a comedy. *Richard III* is not quite a comedy, but neither is it a tragedy. Typically a Shakespearean comedy proliferates confusion of plot and character with the implied promise of a wondrous resolution that delightfully enlarges the field of play in the end. *Richard III* generates the confusions, the contradictions, and through the dazzling con-man artistry of Richard seems to promise (like Falstaff, caught between his wit and his grossness) a marvelous payoff. But it is a pseudocomedy, dead-end comedy. Behind the fiction of Richard versus the World lies the myth of Richard's centrality, a center of power. The struggle is a fantasy; Margaret is a fantastic opposite, Richard's victims are ghosts, and the scenes of encounters are setups, discrete occasions for Richard's mastery of shadows all-too-willing to disappear.

> This is the day wherein I wished to fall
> By the false faith of him whom most I trusted.
>
> (5.1.16–17)

Behind the antithetical structure is a solipsistic need for full control.

I do not speak of *Richard's* need, for that would presume a psychologically complete character, whereas I think we are merely teased by the theatrical gestures of one. But through Richard—through the myth of his centrality and coherence—a fantasy of power is played out. For credibility, it needs the pseudocomic antithetical structure. Yet this structure, and hence Richard's control, are twice severely threatened. The first occasion is Clarence's account of his dream (1.4). Unlike Stanley's dream of the wild boar (3.3) with its obviously flat significations, and certainly unlike Richard's ghostly visitation before Bosworth, Clarence's dream narrative gives form to an unrestrained and continuous flow of feeling. It takes its form not from a convention of moral allegory—the homiletic acceptance of one's guilt because one is found out by the cosmic polygraph—but as images vulcanized from a psyche beset by guilt and terror. The sea-vision is wondrous and ambiguous, and the stifled soul rendered with bodily directness:

> often did I strive
> To yield the ghost; but still the envious flood
> Stopped in my soul, and would not let it forth
> To find the empty, vast, and wand'ring air,
> But smothered it within my panting bulk,
> Who almost burst to belch it in the sea.
>
> (1.4.36–41)

Temporarily the speech is the speaker, just as the dream was the dreamer and not a discrete part in a morality. In its organic unity, and consequently in its dramatic potency, this language opposes itself both to Richard's parodic style and to the rhetorically demonstrative styles of his victims. This alternative is the rare and momentary surfacing, into haunting lyrical images, of a flow of dramatic energy that usually lies concealed within the forms it empowers, but which here, under pressure of obliteration, reveals itself. In other words, the dream narrative suggests a kind of recreative power language might have, but which is systematically smothered in *Richard III*. It does not recur. Clearly it is a kind of language that Richard cannot pervert through parody, and so it makes an independent bid for our attention and engagement that must be suppressed. Richard had warned the murderers not to let Clarence talk; now he must be both stabbed *and* drowned. The need to suppress him speaks for itself.

Clarence personally makes no special claims on us—only his voice—and Richard in the next scene performs upon Edward and the court politicians—newly "reconciled" in peace and love—with such brilliantly extravagant virtuosity that the threat seems to be turned aside. The other challenge to his control of the comic structure comes later: the murder of the young princes. Here, the play's chief way of dealing with the threat of emotional impact is to distance us from the murders. Tyrrel is hired by Richard and in turn hires Dighton and Forrest, whose account of the murder Tyrrel relays in a highly mannered monologue. This comes at a time when Richard's control, both over his own persona and over others, is disintegrating, and it shows him, now king, insulated from the world rather than bustling in it. It presses in on him, visible and immobile at the center, and his agents enact his will badly or not at all. In short, though the play maneuvers to intercept the threat of our engagement in the pathos of the princes, it also pulls away from Richard. In serving his interests—in responding to the need for central control—it exposes the nature of those interests. As in the *Henry VI* plays, but with much steeper articulation, we are disengaged and left to look with chill regard upon the helpless course of the last two acts.

It is not the "success" of Margaret's play of retributive justice—nothing due its power or authority either as drama or as idea—that leads to the debacle of the ending, but the failure of Richard's play: its internal collapse. His compulsive drive toward individuation, the clear antithetical form, has been a continuing testament to his control, but it leads ironically to a high degree of visibility. He uses up the "world"—that is, those shadows who would rather succumb to Margaret's "justice" than incriminate Richard by acting a shrewd audience. He wins the crown, that symbol of the summit of individuation. But then as a Self, rather than an exploiter of others' self-abnegations, Richard turns out to have very little force or coherence. To act directly, visibly, through one's agents, is quite different from acting invisibly through the secret wills of others.

The interview with Queen Elizabeth crystallizes Richard's exhaustion. The scene parodies his seduction of Anne, which of course was a virtuoso performance, brisk and graceful in its immaculate control. Never, before or after, was it clear that Richard really needed Anne for worldly ambitions; the success itself was certainly the point. By contrast stands his *need* for Elizabeth, which keeps him visible as an actor striving but unable to deploy himself in credible shapes of language, figured in his tongue. Moreover, he is (as artist) faced with disintegrating materials. Dissociated from his true object—Elizabeth's unseen, unknown daughter—he is forced to improvise, in Elizabeth, an agent. But he has already used her up; except for her daughter, she has nothing left to lose, to masquerade. Now it is he (as before it was Anne) who labors after a shifting target, while Elizabeth, relentlessly ironic, leads him through a mocking chase after a suitable "title" for his wooing. "There is no other way, / Unless thou couldst put on some other shape, / And not be Richard that hath done all this" (4.4.285–87). As the antic, Richard *has* been able to reshape himself convincingly, in role after role, throughout the play. But the strenuous effort of this interview brings him nothing but himself, "Richard that hath done all this"—that is, the historical Richard that presumably underlay his antic character all along. The disclosure leads directly into a display of incoherence among his followers, "songs of death" from the field, then to Bosworth and Richmond.

This progress toward dramatic exhaustion, the drama's mortification by the "fixed future" of history, magnifies that in *2 Henry VI* where York bid to refashion "history" in his own image and ended up as its fodder. When men fail to re-create they become creatures of the chaos that, in the histories, wears the face of an orthodoxy that is both blindly aggressive and profoundly passive. Margaret's confidence is borne out by the clanking machinery of the final act: the parade of ghosts declaiming Richard's outstanding debts, the reflex-insurgence of a faceless Richmond (Henry Tudor, materializing from overseas—i.e., "out there" again), the colorless correct oration of this blank hero to his troops (which exactly reverses the bookkeeping logic of Margaret's play, as in "If you do fight against your country's foes, / Your country's fat shall pay your pains the hire"), and finally the summary perfection of his closing choric speech. In other words, though Richmond thematically supersedes Margaret as the Nemesis figure, dramatically the last act recapitulates the salient features of her world-theater: strictly sequential, reactive, depersonalized, boasting offstage authority, asserting no intrinsic force or presence. Such drama depends upon the validity of an orthodox context of belief; it would cast *us* as upholders of such a convention, repositories of its authority. If we are even half-willing to play such a role, it must be because Richard as a credible dramatic force has failed. The paralysis of his waking soliloquy shows this. It is not just that he suffers despair, but that he has no means to express his terror other than the frantic manipulation of conventional tropes:

> What do I fear? Myself? There's none else by.
> Richard loves Richard: that is, I am I.
> Is there a murderer here? No. Yes, I am:
> Then fly. What, from myself?
>
> (5.3.183–86)

His charismatic resurgence of energy in the end—his colorfully vicious oration and the dead-end heroics in battle—only underscores the way he has lapsed into the predetermined, the "historical" role as villain.

Richard's dramatic style, by which he remains invisible among his fellows, binds him to them as a parasite on shadows. For three acts he draws blank checks on our all-too-willing credulity. He "stays alive" theatrically so long as he does not succumb to that "historical" character that lies waiting for him like a net under an aerialist. We sustain him with our credulity, hoping that he will dance something new into being, trying to forget the dreary net beneath. The net is the orthodox providential structure of the play; Richard defies it and we cheer, but at last there is nowhere to go, no real risks have been taken and nothing new been produced, and it claims him. Curiously, the historical figure he becomes in his fall is a denial of history, at least of a meaning to history that Shakespeare has been seeking. His fall proclaims the triumph of the More-Holinshed-Tudor myth of history—of that monolithic image of the providence-driven past that Shakespeare has been resisting. Now it looks as if Shakespeare has, like Richard, been operating on the ghostly Providence all along, as his secret security, and so has been binding his powers to it.

Peter Brook, writing of Grotowski, states that "the act of performance is an act of sacrifice, of sacrificing what most men prefer to hide—this is [the actor's] gift to the spectator" (*The Empty Space*). All the signs of such a sacrifice are in Richard's attitudes toward us—the seeming disclosure of original pain, the teasing possibility of a "moral sentience" that in defeat would make him tragic. Like any actor, but magnified, Richard seems powerful because he seems to fetch some "terrific" energy from outside the play's fictional domain and his function in it. Such an "outside" is, paradoxically, an "inside"—an interior and independent "self" that sets him apart from his fictive fellows (to whom this "self" is a ghost, invisible), and that brings him thrusting directly into our presence, a delight and a menace. When it becomes clear that Richard's is only an illusion of such energy, that it is reflected from the fictive world he mocks, that he is its antitype, and that he has no reservoir of secret strength to spend in our presence—that "he" has never been among "us" at all—then he loses his privileged power of ghostliness and becomes an interesting dramatic fiction: netted, and now either edible or analyzable. And indeed, Richard's sacrificial gestures in our direction have been ruses; the parody of intercourse enacted with Anne has been enacted with us as well. He does offer, however, no small attraction—the fantasy (which we may share for a while) of ever-expanding power exercised from an ever-un-broached, unimplicated center, requiring no relinquishing of the gratified self. It is the child's Superman vision projected into a real political world (and no doubt the idea of the artist as superman tempted Shakespeare no less than Marlowe in the brave new theater world of the early 1590s). At the center sits a hypothetical "self," extending control through murderous performance, sustaining itself on our consenting credulity, meanwhile acting to cancel all bonds, to sedate all live engagement, to gather an emptied world all to himself to bustle in. When Richard does disintegrate he discloses no hidden "self," but a set of stunted potentialities: a lack of bustle. Nothing has been sacrificed, and nothing, no "self," created.

What of our role in all this? We are flattered perhaps to analyze our responses in terms of a double-gratification: we enjoy a moral holiday in Richard's antics, and then, William Toole writes, "as the play progresses this faculty [moral judgment] is reawakened and we find the appropriateness of what happens to Richard appealing to our moral instincts." But I suspect our participation in the play is more complicated than this; that this is a kind of rationalized fiction of what really happens. The play inescapably mirrors its audience. The offer of a "sacrifice" by an actor to a spectator is obviously a two-way gesture, frightening as well as exhilarating to the spectator. Something is being required of us too, taken from us in exchange. At the most obvious level we are put under an obligation to think and feel in certain ways, to care, to pay attention, to keep a trust; our freedom is restricted, we are fixed and identified in a special relationship. More profoundly, it is likely that such an exchange in the theater activates its primitive powers to disturb us fundamentally. If we look we lose ourselves because we see something magical. Like Pentheus in *The Bacchae* we both want to look and are afraid, afraid perhaps that looking in itself will entail *our* sacrifice.

We mirror Richard's sham sacrifice, his sham openness. As he pretends to reveal, we pretend to look, to protect what we see. The play becomes a screen where we and Richard are immensely pleased to enact a restricted fiction about history. We reflect his disengagement, his self-protectiveness; in the end, our cover blown, we are expelled from the fictional space, the place of spurious magic. But we leave secretly relieved, glad not to have been asked to be more deeply moved. On the other hand, neither have we been bedazzled by the claims of the theater, and we may be sorry after all to have gotten off so well intact. Richard's own refusal to relinquish control of the play's action has kept us, in turn, free of any real responsibility of feeling for him. When he does at last lose control, he does not gain new power, there is no release of energy (as in *Richard II*, or in any of the tragedies) because there has been nothing growing and seeking the sacrificial action. In the fantasy of control that we share with Richard and with the latent performing mode of the play lies a fear of being changed, of participation in the other, the Not-me. In this mode, the object of acting is to stop others' acting; to murder the bonds of breath as Richard instructs Buckingham to "murder thy breath in middle of a word." Buckingham acts (in 3.3) to conjure support from London crowds for the murder of Hastings. In truth *we* are the prize, to control us the object of the larger performance. But we are approached by a villain, the machiavel's instructor, smiling, with murder figured in his tongue: we must be sedated. Yet moral recoil is hardly warranted here, for we have shared in the process, playing our own self-protective, hence manipulating part, aggressive in our nodding passivity, refusing to mingle breath, to recreate; smiling back at the dancing clown while holding tight to our net.

Military Oratory in *Richard III*

R. Chris Hassel, Jr.

Though Richmond's victory over Richard Hunchback at Bosworth Field
was memorialized in chronicle and verse throughout the sixteenth century,
the question of the aesthetic victory in Shakespeare's *Richard III* remains
alive. Are Richmond's orations to his troops as aesthetically unsatisfying
as some of his most vocal critics claim? Are they "flat," "stiff," "pious,"
and "platitudinous?" Or are they instead ringing assertions of what is right
and just, powerful enough to circumscribe even Richard's dramatic and
rhetorical power? Does the "artist in evil" continue to beguile us, even as
he falls? Or does God's chosen Richmond drown Richard's book, even as
he takes his crown? Because the interpretive questions involve at least two
non disputanda, questions of taste and questions of doctrine, the issue is unlikely ever to be resolved. That adds to its fascination.

I

The influential treatises of Niccolò Machiavelli, [Matthew] Sutcliffe,
Barnabe Rich, and others on the art of war often address the topic of military oratory. They therefore become a useful Renaissance prism through
which we can view and try to judge the relative attractiveness of Richmond and Richard during their controversial final scenes.

In *The Art of War* Machiavelli calls a good oratorical style essential to
military leadership:

From *Shakespeare Quarterly* 35, no. 1 (Spring 1984). © 1984 by the Folger Shakespeare Library.

> It was requisite that the excellente Capitaines were oratours: for
> that without knowyng how to speake to al the army, with dif-
> ficultie male be wrought any good thing. . . . This speakyng
> taketh awaie feare, incourageth the mindes, increaseth the obsti-
> natenes to faight, discovereth the deceiptes, promiseth re-
> wardes, sheweth the perilles, and the waie to avoide theim,
> reprehendeth, praieth, threateneth, filleth full of hope, praise,
> shame, and doeth all those thynges, by the whiche the humaine
> passions are extincte, or kendled.

Machiavelli's contemporaries add such crucial particulars as the effective
exploitation of God and good cause, and the favorable interpretation of
signs. They say that a military leader should stress the weaknesses of the
foe and the potency of the leader's own valiant past. Finally he should invoke love of captain and of country.

In *A Distant Mirror*, Barbara Tuchman discusses the importance of
God and of just cause in medieval and early Renaissance warfare.

> While desirable in any epoch, a 'just war' in the 14th century
> was virtually a legal necessity as the basis for requisitioning feu-
> dal aids in men and money. It was equally essential for securing
> God on one's side, for war was considered fundamentally an
> appeal to the arbitrement of God.

Matthew Sutcliffe's influential military manual begins with a lengthy
argument for just cause: "first, I require religion," he says, for "God he is
Lord of Hostes, and giver of victories; and sure it is not probable, he will
give it to those, that aske it not at his handes." Elsewhere Sutcliffe writes
that the "General [must] be religious, and a mainteiner of religion, . . . if
hee expect the favour of God, and good successe in his affaires." In other
Renaissance military manuals the appeal to God and good cause can smack
as much of opportunism as it does of piety. Onosander suggests that "the
sugred talke of the Captaine maye move thym . . . unto great actes for the
love of vertue." Machiavelli writes, "Enterprises maie the safelier be
brought to passe by meanes of religion." Machiavelli even advises citing
dreams as evidence of God's favor, whether or not they have occurred:

> Many have tolde how God hath appered unto them in their
> slepe, who hath admonished them to faight. In our fathers
> time, Charles the seventh kyng of Fraunce, in the warre whiche
> he made againste the Englishemen, saied, he counsailed with a

maide, sent from God, . . . the which was occasion of his victorie.

Whether pious or practical, the invocation of God and just cause was an essential weapon in the arsenal of the military orator.

II

Though with none of this cynicism, Richmond can honestly and effectively report to his captains:

> Me thought their Soules, whose bodies *Richard* murther'd
> Came to my Tent, and cried on Victory:
> I promise you my Heart is very jocond,
> In the remembrance of so faire a dreame
>
> (ll. 3695–98)

We have seen these souls and heard their unanimous testimony that "God, and our good cause, fight upon our side" (l. 3706).

Think how often the motif occurs. "Vertuous and holy be thou Conqueror," says the ghost of Henry VI. "Good Angels guard thy battell, Live and Flourish," says Clarence. The two young princes bless Richmond: "Good Angels guard thee from the Boares annoy." Richard's Anne promises: "Thou quiet soule, / Sleep thou a quiet sleepe: / Dreame of Successe, and Happy Victory." Buckingham completes this chorus affirming God and good cause: "God, and good Angels fight on *Richmonds* side" (ll. 3575–3636, passim). Richmond and his allies often claim God and good cause in their military oratory. They march "In Gods name, cheerely on." Their good "Conscience is a thousand men" (ll. 3419–27, passim). Richmond is assured of God and good cause in his devout prayer and in his battle oration (ll. 3551–57, 3706–36). When Richmond reminds his men of these two potent allies, we know that he is telling the truth as well as exploiting an effective first strategy of military oratory. Richmond and his forces believe in God and just cause. They believe in their opponent's depravity. In the last battle they are strengthened in these beliefs.

Richard, in sharp contrast, can neither shake off the horrifying effects of his dream of despair and death nor dissemble otherwise before his allies:

> O Ratcliffe, I have dreamd a fearefull dreame,
> What thinkst thou, will our friendes prove all true?
>
> (ll. 3674–75)

> By the Apostle *Paul*, shadowes to night
> Have stroke more terror to the soule of *Richard*,
> Then can the substance of ten thousand Souldiers
> Armed in proofe, and led by shallow *Richmond*.
>
> (ll. 3677–80)

Again we have witnessed the unanimous testimony of the ghosts. As Richard knows, it is more substance than shadow. He has stabbed a king, butchered two princes, punched another king "full of holes," washed a brother to death, killed Rivers, Grey, Vaughan, Hastings, "wretched *Anne*," and Buckingham. His cause is overwhelmingly bad; all of these "wrongs" are in Richard's bosom, weighing him down like lead. "Bloody and guilty" becomes the countering epithet to Richmond's "Vertuous and holy"—that and "dispaire and dye." Near the middle of this chorus, all chant to Richmond, "Awake, / And thinke our wrongs in *Richards* bosome, / Will conquer him. Awake, and win the day" (ll. 3564–95, passim).

Not only is Richard without supernatural sanction or good cause for the upcoming battle; he is also without the wit or the will to pretend to have them. This is true when he wakes; it is also true during his battle oration. Not incidentally, Hall's Richard is more than equal to this challenge. Shakespeare's is not. Apparently he knows that he is "One that hath ever beene Gods Enemy." Richmond's corollary is inescapable: "Then if you fight against Gods Enemy, / God will in justice ward you as his Souldiers" (ll. 3718–20). Only Richmond can invoke such an ally in Shakespeare's version of the battle orations or during the final act. By any standards, then—whether Sutcliffe's idealism or Machiavelli's cynicism—Richard is Richmond's clear inferior in terms of God and good cause. He does not even invoke them as an oratorical technique.

III

On the other hand, Richard is probably better than Richmond at the time-honored strategy of putting down his enemy, even though Richmond has better material to work with. Machiavelli advises his military orator to "make thy men to esteme little the enemie, as Agesilao a Spartaine used, who shewed to his souldiou[r]s, certain Persians naked, to the intent that seyng their delicate members, thei should not have cause to feare them." Sutcliffe suggests declaring "the enemies wantes, and weakenes, and disadvantages." Harault cites the example of Lisander at the siege of Corinth, who said to his troops, "Are you not ashamed to be afraid to assaile those enemies, which are so slothfull and negligent, that hares sleep quietly within the precinct of their walles."

Richard's speech is composed almost exclusively of such deprecation of his enemies. He insults Richmond's troops:

> Remember whom you are to cope withall,
> A sort of Vagabonds, Rascals, and Run-awayes,
> A scum of Brittaines, and base Lackey Pezants,
> Whom their o're-cloyed Country vomits forth
> To desperate Adventures, and assur'd Destruction.
> (ll. 3785–89)

He calls them "straglers," "over-weening Ragges of France," "famish'd Beggars," "poore Rats," "bastard Britaines" (ll. 3785–3803, passim). He insults Richmond in the same key:

> And who doth leade them, but a paltry Fellow?
> Long kept in Britaine at our Mothers cost,
> A Milke-sop, one that never in his life
> Felt so much cold, as over shooes in Snow.
> (ll. 3793–96)

Without just cause or God's name, Richard's recourse to this tactic smacks of desperation and of pettiness. But he does play this Machiavellian card for all it is worth.

Richmond is not totally deficient, incidentally, in this strategy. Against Richard he says,

> For, what is he they follow? Truly Gentlemen,
> A bloudy Tyrant, and a Homicide:
> One rais'd in blood, and one in blood establish'd;
> One that made meanes to come by what he hath,
> And slaughter'd those that were the meanes to help him:
> A base foule Stone, made precious by the soyle
> Of Englands Chaire, where he is falsely set:
> One that hath ever beene Gods Enemy.
> (ll. 3711–17)

Earlier, Richmond had also attacked Richard as

> The wretched, bloody, and usurping Boare,
> (That spoyl'd your Summer Fields, and fruitfull Vines)

> Swilles your warm blood like wash, & makes his trough
> In your embowel'd bosomes: This foule Swine.
>
> (ll. 3412–15)

Both speakers, then, use this tactic freely. The differences in their usage deserve notice. A fourth of Richmond's military oratory is *ad hominem*, as against nearly three-fourths of Richard's. Further, Richmond's assaults against Richard are mostly true. That is to say, they are not so much *ad hominem* argument as articulations of just cause; witness the deserved final epithets as "Gods Enemy." That Richard speaks *ad hominem* almost exclusively attests further to his loss of wit and vitality at this crucial moment. He himself admits "I have not that Alacrity of Spirit, / Nor cheere of Minde that I was wont to have" (ll. 3513–14). In Richmond's mouth, attacking the man asserts Richard's unjust cause. Paradoxically, it may also add some attractive dents of humanity to the surface of Richmond's shining armor. Shakespeare follows Hall more closely in this respect than in others. Perhaps he too wanted that healthy dose of anger, which sometimes "hath a privilege" even in God's minister.

Incidentally, Richard may also take his own oratory too literally here. Harault advises against overconfidence before battle, a fault Richard betrays in his oration. Of Darius's defeat by Alexander, he says: "The thing that undid him, was his overweening opinion that he should overcome Alexander with ease, which is the thing that overthroweth all such as upon disdain to their enemies, do set no good order in their affairs, and in the leading of their armies." Richmond's oration acknowledges the military power as well as the moral impotence of his foe.

IV

As further advice, Sutcliffe urges the military orator "to confirme them with hope and report of their former valiant actions." Garrard stresses "the example of magnanimitie in their forefathers." Richard has the better of Richmond in this area. He can effectively remind his troops of the battles of Poitiers and Crecy and Agincourt, all major English victories over the French: "And not these bastard Britaines; whom our Fathers / Have in their owne Land beaten, bobb'd, and thump'd, / And on Record, left them the heires of shame" (ll. 3803–5). Richard's troops should be encouraged that they are again engaging these French. In the light of recent history, Richmond's men must be more than a little unsure.

In fact, Richmond might be countering that fear by leaning so heavily on God's help and on the theme of hope: "In Gods name cheerely on, couragious Friends, / To reape the Harvest of perpetuall peace, / By this one bloody tryall of sharpe Warre." Again he urges, "Then in Gods name march, / True Hope is swift, and flyes with Swallowes wings, / Kings it makes Gods, and meaner creatures Kings." Even at the end of his oration, he encourages them similarly, "Sound Drummes and Trumpets boldly, and cheerefully, / God and Saint *George, Richmond,* and Victory." Without the precedent of recent victory, Richmond must emphasize his good hope in God's cause and their own. He must encourage them as Englishmen, invoking St. George. His reassurances have a psychological validity, an insight into human nature and human need, an awareness of his own vulnerability and that of his troops, that further humanize Richmond. Like Hal inspiring the troops before Agincourt, Richmond is effective because he is one of them. They are truly "Fellowes in Armes," and "most loving Frends" (ll. 3406–29, passim; 3735–36). Richmond may thus turn this apparent disadvantage to his favor; in the process he becomes a more attractive character as well.

V

With "Encourage them with promises, and hope of rewarde," Sutcliffe sounds another common theme of military oratory. Garrard urges reciting "benefits to soule and bodie," crisply combining the appeal to greed with that to just cause. Machiavelli says that any good orator "promiseth rewardes." Interestingly, Richmond is much more lavish than Richard in numbering the rewards of battle. However, Shakespeare has refined his appeal considerably from that recounted in Hall:

> Therefore labour for your gayne and swet for your right: while we were in Brytaine we had small livynges and litle plentye of welth or welfare, now is the tyme come to get abundance of riches and copie of profit, which is the reward of your service and merite of your payne.

Shakespeare's Richmond replaces material gain with these nobler spoils:

> Then if you fight against Gods Enemy,
> God will in justice ward you as his Soldiers.
> If you do sweare to put a Tyrant downe,
> You sleepe in peace, the Tyrant being slaine:
> If you do fight against your Countries Foes,
> Your Countries Fat shall pay your paines the hyre.

> If you do fight in safegard of your wives,
> Your wives shall welcome home the Conquerors.
> If you do free your Children from the Sword,
> Your Childrens Children quits it in your Age.
>
> (ll. 3719–28)

God's reward, peaceful sleep, a welcome home, love, honor in old age—
these are the rewards of noble combat in Richmond's good cause. "Coun-
tries Fat" is his one concession to the more materialistic interests of his
men. Even Brutus would not be embarrassed by this Cassius.

Richard, being in power, leans instead on threats to the *status quo*, fear
of shame and fear of loss:

> You sleeping safe, they bring you to unrest:
> You having Lands, and blest with beauteous wives,
> They would restraine the one, distaine the other.
>
> (ll. 3790–92)

Lost lands, stained wives, unrest—these are the threats of the established
but reeling King. "Shall these enjoy our Lands? lye with our Wives? / Rav-
ish our daughters?" (ll. 3806–7). The repetition again suggests desperation.
It also betrays a lack of cause and a loss of ingenuity, not to mention a
dearth of abstract value in Richard's universe. On the other hand, all of
these arguments are also established parts of the arsenal of military oratory. Sutcliffe says, "Feare them with shame." Machiavelli and Garrard
urge threatening "present peril." Richard uses what little stock he has.
However, his inventory of invention is running almost as low as the number of causes he can claim.

VI

Of "love of Captain and country" we must infer the effectiveness of
Richard and Richmond from their words and from the responses of their
men. Both leaders invoke the patriotic hero and patron saint of England,
St. George. Richmond connects him with God, Richard with "the spleene
of fiery Dragons" (l. 3822). Hope and despair are fairly obviously the respective companions of Richmond and Richard in this little counterpoint.
Both men harp on defending their land, their wives, and their children.
Richard can have little moral leverage with the last two points. Richmond
addresses "most loving Friends" and "loving Countrymen," and seems
surrounded by them in Oxford, Blount, Herbert, and Stanley. Richard has

Surrey, Norfolk, Ratcliffe, and Catesby, loyal chiefs if not loving friends. But when Blount says "He hath no friends, but what are friends for fear" (l. 3425), we cannot believe him far wrong. Richard addresses no friends in his oration, only the "Gentlemen of England" (l. 3809). Their only true cause is country, not king. Even the diminished Richard is apparently aware of this liability in his words of address.

VII

Elaborate signs precede the battle, and the public reactions of Richard and Richmond to them are instructive. Proctor says, "some people doe stumble muche at sygnes or tokens which befall before battaill, . . . wherefore the wyse captayne will chearefullye expounde all suche chaunces for his advauntage . . . [as] a happy sygne of the victorye fallinge unto him." Richmond has an easy time of this, because his signs are good and his heart is jocund. He has had "the sweetest sleepe, / And fairest boading Dreames, / That ever entred in a drowsie head." The ghosts have promised "Successe, and Happy Victory." Therefore Richmond does not have to feign when he cheerfully proclaims, "Me thought their Soules, whose bodies *Richard* murther'd, / Came to my Tent, and cried on Victory" (ll. 3623, 3691–96, passim).

Richard does have to feign good cheer, and he cannot. His vaunted ingenuity fails him yet again, as it has failed him consistently ever since he became king. To Ratcliffe he admits, "I have dreamd a fearefull dreame." He adds, "shadowes to night / Have stroke more terror to the soule of *Richard*, / Then can the substance of ten thousand Souldiers / Armed in proofe, and led by shallow *Richmond*." To the troops there is a similar admission, only barely masked by ineffective bravado: "Let not our babling Dreames affright our soules: / For Conscience is a word that Cowards use." Unless all of his troops are as cynical, as skeptical, as Richard himself, this piece of oratory does not augur well for his cause, or speak well of his presence of mind. Richmond ignores the darkling sky. Richard is enveloped by it, as by guilt: "Who saw the Sunne today?" he asks; "Then he disdaines to shine . . . . A blacke day will it be to somebody." All of this is spoken out loud, before Ratcliffe and Catesby. Then "The Sun will not be seene to day, / The sky doth frowne, and lowre upon our Army. / I would these dewy teares were from the ground." Even when Richard rouses himself to shake off the omen, he still attests unconsciously to its power: "the selfe-same Heaven / That frownes on me, lookes sadly upon him" (ll. 3674 and 1–3779, passim).

Heaven frowns on Richard; on Richmond it looks sadly. They are not the same. Richard knows it, and he cannot feign otherwise. The good face that he puts on immediately afterward remains colored gray by these frowning skies. The desperation and emptiness of the oration which follows is darkened too by Richard's encounters with these signs and tokens. His despair must affright the souls of all but the most depraved of his men.

VIII

Finally, Richmond is simply a better orator than Richard. Richard is superb in one-on-one conversations. His soliloquies and his earliest dialogue are masterpieces of personal, colloquial rhetoric, full of energy, wit, and inspiration. But Richard is no public speaker. By nature chaotic, Richard is no good at the ordered, formal flourishes that characterize most good oratory. When he tries to use them, his crude images, downward comparisons, and base epithets are incongruent with the high style. As in so many other ways, Richard as military orator is finally a victim of himself. "What shall I say more than I have inferr'd?" (l. 3784) is an interesting admission of this victimization. Richard has denied God. He has forsaken all traditional values, all abstractions even. "Conscience is a word," says this nominalist, "Air—a trim reckoning." Like Falstaff's "catechism," Richard's comment here dooms him to ultimate impotency. He is himself alone. So his language is limited to his condition of being. After the brief interlude of the Vice, he is base, inferential, uninspiring.

Richmond, in contrast, because he is allied with God and good cause, is eloquent precisely because he is not alone. He believes in God, in virtue, in family, friends, and country; he believes in order, in justice. Shakespeare's Richmond knows truth; he does not infer it. Thus he can assert truth and be believed in that assertion. Richmond exploits this advantage to the hilt, but because he also believes it, there is no dissimulation. Truth arms his oratory. Style and being are one. Richard is no longer clever enough or sufficiently in command of himself to use Richmond's rhetorical strategies, even cynically. Words, so often abused by Richard, continue to take their revenge.

Barnabe Rich says of the captain's oratory that "it encourageth the minds either of hope, either else of despair." There could hardly be a clearer illustration of these opposites than during the battle orations in *Richard III*. Richmond unequivocally ends on the note of hope, as he should since his cause is just and his conscience clear: "Sound Drummes and Trumpets boldly, and cheerefully, / God and Saint *George, Richmond,* and Victory." Richard's strains are much as the ghosts predicted, chaotic, sulphurous, full of valiant fury, signifying nothing. He prefaces his oration, "March on, joyne bravely, let us too't pell mell, / If not to heaven, then hand in hand to Hell." He ends it with "Our Ancient word of Courage, faire S. *George* / Inspire us with the spleene of fiery Dragons: / Upon them, Victorie sits on our helmes" (ll. 3735–36, 3782–83, 3821–23). It does, like a vulture or a leering Beelzebub. St. George is not the dragon, nor is he just a word. If Richard had the time or the composure, even he might appreciate this last revenge of language and truth upon himself.

In the final act of *Richard III*, and in the chronicle tradition too, military oratory consistently, though not simplistically, proves to be one of Richmond's strengths and one of Richard's weaknesses. After Richmond's oration, Hall reports, "These cherefull wordes he sett forthe with such gesture of his body and smylyng countenance, as though all redye he had vanquyshed hys enemies." The effect of Richard's oration was quite different:

> This exhortacion encouraged all such as favoured hym, but suche as were present more for dreade then love, kyssed them openly, whom they inwardely hated other sware outwardely to take part with suche whose death thei secretely compassed and inwardely imagened, other promised to invade the kynge's enemies, whiche fled and fought with fyrce courage against the kyng. . . . So was his people to hym unsure and unfaithfull at his ende.

Shakespeare seems to have followed Hall very closely in these respects. Richard's battle oration simply did not work, in Hall or in Shakespeare. "So was his people to hym unsure and unfaithfull at his ende." The murderous Machiavelli could have schooled Richard better on military oratory. But then, there was no "good thing" that Richard could have wrought by the final scene of his life, except his death.

According to the standards of the foremost military manuals of the time, Richmond overwhelms Richard before the Battle of Bosworth Field. Richard knows the oratorical rules, but his speeches remain vacuous and desperate. In contrast, Richmond is a savvy military orator who is also a good man. Further, he has good men to respond to his good words. If God and good cause fight on Richmond's side, so do considerable rhetorical skills. The power of his ordered rhetoric predicts his subsequent success at arms. Richmond's words have been weighed too lightly in the critical and the theatrical traditions. Perhaps filtering them through these military manuals will help to right the balance.

Usurpation, Seduction, and the Problematics of the Proper: A "Deconstructive," "Feminist" Rereading of the Seductions of Richard and Anne

Marguerite Waller

About that title. It strikes me as verbose, pretentious, overly Latinate, ty-pographically busy, and quite probably off-putting. But I do not know how else to indicate to you or to myself what I am trying to do at this moment in a collaborative attempt to reread (or rewrite) the Renaissance from a number of recently conceived political and especially "feminist" positions. I have trouble naming either my topic or my approach, not least because it is a certain violence implicit in naming itself that I want to make available for closer examination. Jacques Derrida, the formulator of the nonname, nonconcept "deconstruction," has argued that it is this violence, a violence of or in language, that underwrites the traditional discourses of reference and meaning in which, as he and several feminist theoreticians have gone on to demonstrate, "woman" always comes off badly. It is this violence that continues to frustrate even the most thorough-going "decon-structive" attempts to open western discourses of knowledge to the dis-courses of women. I place "feminist" and "deconstructive" in quotation marks here and in my title, then, to call attention to this violence, the structure of which we will presently examine in greater detail.

I also want to suggest a second, related, problem. That is, the two terms are not necessarily compatible. They do not signal a harmonious,

From *Rewriting the Renaissance: The Discourses of Sexual Difference in Early Modern Europe,* edited by Margaret W. Ferguson, Maureen Quilligan, and Nancy J. Vick-ers. © 1986 by the University of Chicago. University of Chicago Press, 1986.

homogeneous, coextensive set of concerns and practices. By reading deconstructively I may be able to de-liberalize or refigure the figure "man" so as to show how the speaking, writing, knowing subject of the discourse of knowledge does not itself escape its violent rhetorical origins, how its own status as a linguistic artifact precludes the possibility of its serving as the ground of meaning and being. I might go on, as Derrida has done in *Spurs: Nietzsche's Styles*, to demarcate "man" by means of gender. The issue would then become how the category "man," when it is de-figured, interpreted as literal, comes to operate linguistically in ways that compel gender discrimination. I could point out that "man," seen as working beyond rhetorical determinations, compels the subordination of the category "woman." Woman appears as the dangerous, supplemental, figural term; man as the stable, literal one. She becomes a secondary depriviled entity, an object to be investigated; man the primary term, the subject who performs the investigation. She can be seen only in her relation to men, while men are seen as transcending such networks of relations.

But such deconstructive reading appears unable to ask why it was that man became the unscrutinized term in the first place. And as Gayatri Spivak has recently asked, is the position of woman really being interrogated when the philosopher moves into what he has determined to be her position the better to ask what "man" is? Doesn't the deconstruction of the general sign of man still depend upon the figural determination of woman inherited from what is now seen to be a phallocentric system of thought, and isn't woman, therefore, not better spoken for or about, but doubly displaced, at the very moment when she appears to inaugurate the new regime of quotation marks?

There seems to be a failure, then, of the questions posed by deconstruction and those posed by feminism to match up. Not that this failure necessarily takes the form of an opposition. The nonrelation of deconstruction and feminism to which Spivak points may allow the two to work together fruitfully as demarcations of each other's explanatory limits. The logic of deconstruction suspends the conditions under which it makes sense to ask direct, historical, and epistemological questions (such as, how, when, why did "man" become the subject and referent of our knowledge about, among other things, gender? What does it mean to be a woman? What has it meant and what might it come to mean?). But feminism reminds us that the position of woman in language, by its very difference from "man's," "means" that "man's" discourse, even in the form offered by Derrida, which strives toward ending the centrality of "man," has its own particular kind of boundary. Not that we can "know" something about "woman" that goes unproblematized by deconstruction's insights into discourse, but that between deconstructive and feminist logic there now emerges the event of their "missed encounter." That is, the nonconfrontation between deconstruction and feminism can be seen as an event (although an event of a different order from that constituted by traditional epistemology) accessible as a historical reality. As Shoshana Felman suggests in a canny analysis (from which I have just been drawing) of J. L. Austin's speech act theory and its comparable discontinuities with continental linguistic thought, such misfires, instances of the impossibility of translating from one argument into another, give us a different kind of referent to consider—what she calls a "material knowledge of language." Such knowledge, Felman stresses, "has to do with reality" because referential knowledge about language "is itself—at least in part—what this reality is made of." But this referent is conceived of as an act, that is a dynamic movement of modification of reality. The quotation marks in my title are intended to evoke this kind of successful failure, one that performs an act modifying rather than reinforcing the reality suggested by either approach in the absence of the other. In the context of a reading of seduction scenes in Shakespeare's *Richard III*, I would like to think of this act as an antiseduction. As I present my argument—that Shakespeare's characters Richard and Anne and many of the play's commentators are seduced by the dream of a common language in which the radical potential of this heteronomy is suppressed—my commitment is to the subversion of such suppression.

I

Cette fissure n'est pas une fissure parmi d'autres. Elle est la fissure: la nécessité de l'intervalle, la dure loi de l'espacement.
(JACQUES DERRIDA, *De la grammatologie*)

Academic commentators on *Richard III* have found much to admire in the character Richard. He has been called, among other things, "buoyantly vital," "fascinating," "creative," "self-knowing," "a great artist," "a great actor," "a wit," "an ironist," "a human representative, bolder than ourselves, resisting the oppression of history," "a ruthless, demonic comedian with . . . the seductive appeal of an irresistible gusto." By contrast, the female characters within the play refer to him as a "wretch," "a villain slave," "the slave of nature," "a toad," "a bottled spider," "a dissembler," and "the troubler of the poor world's peace." In the slightly more politicized language of the deposed queen, Margaret, he is "that excellent grand tyrant of the earth / That reigns in galled eyes of weeping souls." Were I to judge Richard, a critical gesture that I find of questionable political or epistemological usefulness either to the female figures in the play or to my project, the catalogue of epithets might read as follows: Richard is politically and intellectually stupid, cowardly, and boring. A sentimental writer and reader of himself and of others, he is a relatively common species of manipulative narcissist. My point, however, is not that my position or that of the play's internal critics of Richard is right and the positions of various twentieth-century male (as it happens) critics are wrong. I want to call attention instead to the enormous discrepancy concerning what judgment is to be made of, what value is to be seen in, the figure of Richard. Such discrepancies present us with a dramatic eruption of the kind of violence, an unavoidable violence, that underwrites the making of all moral and aesthetic judgments. It will prove a useful detour in an investigation of seduction—itself, etymologically a leading aside or detour—to turn our attention first to that fundamental violence implicated in this instance of critical disagreement.

Like other kinds of naming, such judgments participate in what Derrida, in an essay on Claude Lévi-Strauss, has called the "violence of the letter." Explicitly in that essay and implicitly throughout his work, Derrida has concerned himself with the structure and effects of the way in which language necessarily effaces or represses its indeterminate origins in the infinite play of phonemic difference. If, as structural linguists maintain, meaning is diacritical, the product of the free play of difference, then in order for words to seem "proper," to appear as stable, self-identical entities endowed with stable meanings, this play of difference must be effaced. The indeterminate origins of linguistic signification must be repressed. It is Derrida's breakdown into stages of this effacement or repression that I have found especially pertinent to the case at hand.

Derrida (or his text, which here performs a little exemplary violence on "proper" French) has termed the first stage the "violence originaire" of language. The term, *originaire* or "originary," not to be found in either the French or the English lexicon, and not meaning "original" or "primary" but something prior to the possibility of such concepts, aptly enacts the way in which a word can never be "proper," literal, only and wholly itself. Derrida's gnarled explication of the term tries to confront and combat our commonsense feel for the order of things as it lays out a different, difficult to conceptualize schema:

> To name, to give names . . . such is the originary violence of
> language which consists in inscribing within a difference, in
> classifying, in suspending the vocative absolute. To think the
> unique *within* the system, to inscribe it there, such is the gesture
> of the arche-writing: arche-violence, loss of the proper, of abso-
> lute proximity, of self-presence, in truth the loss of what has
> never taken place, of a self-presence which has never been
> given but only dreamed of and always already split, repeated,
> incapable of appearing to itself except in its own disappearance.

In other words, names are never simply what they are but are identified by what they are not, as well. The violence done to and through difference by naming works by constituting a presence which then seems to
precede difference. This implies, among other things, that the substantial-
ity that a name "literally" suggests or seems to promise is fundamentally
illusory. There occurs, however, a second, "reparatory" violence, implied
by and inseparable from the first, whereby this "loss of the proper . . . of
what has never been given but only dreamed of" is concealed and compen-
sated for. In a violent rewriting of the originary violence, the "proper"
becomes the proper. Rather than a mere appearance made possible by, but
doing violence to, difference, "literal" meaning comes to appear as itself
the ground from which contraries and conflicts emerge. It is the emer-
gence of these contraries and conflicts in the form of a third violence, empirical violence, that we tend to interpret in moral, legal, and other
evaluative ways. For Derrida, though, this last violence remains unrecu-
perated and anything but neutralized by normative systems of law and
value. Instead, empirical violence refers back to the complex, abyssal
structures of rhetorical violence that underwrite it. Thus, in a way, empirical violence undoes the work of the first two stages. "In effect it reveals
the first nomination which was already an expropriation . . . it denudes
also that which since then functioned as the proper, the so-called proper."
Though not often, and not always advisably, seen this way, war, murder,
rape—and verbal disagreement—violently strip away "the reassuring seal
of self-identity" of nations, person, and ideas.

If, as I have been urging, the attempt to judge Richard's performance
aesthetically or morally in no way escapes this problematics of the proper,
then it should come as no surprise that there are—and had better be—dis-
agreements among such readings. The mistake would be not to expect
such conflicts or to try to resolve or abolish them on the assumption that
this would make one's own critical position secure. Such a gesture would

be structurally analogous to Richard's elimination of everyone who appears to threaten his claim to absolute authority and is magnificently undercut by the irony emplotted in Richard's homicidal progress toward the throne. As he systematically kills off those against whom he defines himself, he fails to understand that the dream of self-identity and self-determination (which he identifies with the throne) necessarily recedes from his grasp. His rhetorical situation just before the end of the play, on the morning of the battle of Bosworth, anticipates what is about to become his empirical situation—nonexistence. Richard says, "I myself / find in myself no pity to myself" (5.3.203–4), echoing the tortured attempt to name the self of Petrarch's famous line—"di me medesmo meco mi vergogno." The play's evocation at this moment of Petrarch's *Canzoniere*, one of the foremost Renaissance investigations of the indeterminate, fragmented situation of the self as it is "known" in and through language, signals just how far off-base Richard's "self-knowledge" has become. His lack of self-knowledge shortly proves fatal. His collision with Richmond on the battlefield gives the lie to his sense of a stable, self-conscious, sovereign subjectivity, proving it no more than a fragile linguistic construct. Had he recognized the provisional nature of the self, he might have chosen to do things differently. As it is, we see him crash blindly against an "enemy" paradoxically generated out of his own ever-increasing need for antagonistic others.

There will be more to say about Richard's unself-conscious use of Petrarchan discourse later, but first, let me complete the analogy between Richard's usurptive position and a certain kind of position-taking by literary critics. This time my point of departure is the emphasis placed by two feminist critics, Madonne Miner and Irene Dash, on the extent to which male-authored performances of and commentaries on *Richard III* have almost completely overlooked, and invariably subordinated, the women in the play, even though only female characters undergo significant changes in outlook and feeling. As the seemingly endless pattern of usurpations in the *Henry VI* and *Richard III* tetralogy systematically destroys their legal, emotional, and biological bonds to men, Elizabeth and Margaret give up the competitive backbiting of the latter play's first act, and, in act 4, together with Richard's mother, they collaboratively redefine their positions in precisely the terms to which Richard's mode of self-definition blinds him—in terms, namely, of the instability of identity that their losses have brought them to acknowledge. Margaret, especially, can see not only the fact, but the positive advantages of such instability, preferring to become a Shakespearean prototype of the "new French feminist" than to stay in the English court. To Elizabeth she announces:

> Now thy proud neck bears half my burdened
> yoke,
> From which even here I slip my wearied head
> And leave the burden of it all on thee.
> Farewell, York's wife, and queen of sad mischance!
> These English woes shall make me smile in France.
> (4.4.111–15)

This scene has been criticized for being "impersonal," "mainly ritual," and "rigidly formalized," and has often been cut from performances. The passages of lamentation in which Richards and Edwards become indistinguishable as murderers and victims, usurpers and usurped, are found to be particularly objectionable. The recognition that these characters *are* fundamentally self-destructive and structurally indistinguishable, then, does not occur. Nor can the scene lend its support to Coppélia Kahn's theory that the means whereby the male characters know and define themselves is very much at issue in the play. By subordinating this scene, or leaving it out of account, one misses the contrast, for example, between Margaret's farewell speech and Richard's hectic defense of his identity, his inability or unwillingness to slip its burden: "What do I fear? Myself? There's none else by. / Richard loves Richard: that is, I am I" (5.3.183–84). On a larger scale, one misses the relation between Richard's discourse in the first part of the play, his so-called "creative," "self-knowing," soliloquies and manipulations, and his subsequent disintegration and defeat. The turn of events then has to be accounted for with such critical constructs as "the Tudor myth of history," "a divine moral plan," or some other arbitrary check to what is perceived as Richard's power. Clearly this is the feminist in me talking. My dislike of this particular critical reduction or misreading (and every reading, for by now obvious reasons, will be partial) has everything to do with my "being" a feminist woman. The deconstructionist in me, however, no less urgently, wants to call attention to the failure of this position to acknowledge the *illusoriness* (not the "wrongness") of its ground. It is in this sense that, intentionally or not, such a position participates in and perpetuates Richard's politics—sexual and other.

The feminist reader is, I hasten to elaborate, just as subject to the problematics of the proper as are the more traditional critics upon whose texts I have been commenting. If one assumes that the women in the play would be all right were it not for their dependence upon the power and privilege of their fathers, husbands, brothers, and sons, one may be poorly placed to investigate the levels of sheerly rhetorical violence to which this arrangement complexly refers. Put another way, the dream of a female self that appears to itself as autonomous and authoritative as the male selves of Shakespeare's Lancastrian and Yorkist courts would sustain rather than undermine the kinds of position the male characters in the play are portrayed as occupying. It is precisely her susceptibility to this dream, in fact, that dooms Lady Anne. In order to analyze the part played in the extinction of *both* Richard and Anne, not only by male supremacy and misogyny but also by an essentializing discourse that may be employed by either sex, it becomes important not to take these characters' word either for themselves or for the social organization within which we see them embedded, but to examine closely the rhetorical structure of the characters' language about themselves. It then becomes possible to begin to describe how these selves, as they are rhetorically constituted, interlock with one another and how they are related to the usurpations and seductions that figure so largely in this play. Why is it, for example, that Richard can contemplate usurpations by others with irony, but, nevertheless, feel compelled unironically to perpetrate one of his own? Why, if Lady Anne is already at the mercy of her politically antagonistic suitor (repeating the pattern of the two queens, Margaret and Elizabeth, in the *Henry VI* plays), is Richard drawn to commit the apparently gratuitous violence of making her abandon her personal and emotional, as well as her political allegiances? My hope is not that we shall then be in a better position from which to indulge in such self-aggrandizing gestures as judging Richard and Anne or the social structures portrayed in the play but that this Renaissance text, among others, may become a more active site of the cultural self-critique with which both deconstruction and feminism, however asynchronously, are currently engaged.

II

It is not simply a question of literature's ability to say or not to say the truth of sexuality. For from the moment literature begins to try to set things straight on that score, literature itself becomes inextricable from the sexuality it seeks to comprehend.

BARBARA JOHNSON, *The Critical Difference*

The seduction of Anne, the occasion that has generated most of the positive commentary on Richard, is not, I would maintain, the first seduction in the play. In the opening soliloquy of act 1, Richard's own discourse enacts a kind of leading aside or away from one's own cause very similar to that which occurs to Anne in the second scene. It will be important, then, to attend closely to the means of self-definition—or as I would prefer to call it, self-seduction—in the opening scene, before trying to determine who does what to whom in scene 2. The soliloquy begins with a memorable but ironic catalogue of the antitheses presented by the "peacetime" court of Edward IV (Richard's brother) to the civil strife it replaces:

> Now is the winter of our discontent
> Made glorious summer by this sun of York
> And all the clouds that loured upon our house
> In the deep bosom of the ocean buried.
>
> (1.1.1–4)

As the antitheses pile up, Richard wittily compresses the oppositions into single lines:

> Now are our brows bound with victorious wreaths,
> Our bruised arms hung up for monuments,
> Our stern alarum changed to merry meetings,
> Our dreadful marches to delightful measures.
> Grim-visaged War hath smoothed his wrinkled front.
>
> (1.1.5–9)

and then formulates a longer, more involved contrast:

> And now, instead of mounting barbed steeds
> To fright the souls of fearful adversaries
> He capers nimbly in a lady's chamber
> To the lascivious pleasing of a lute.
>
> (1.1.10–13)

These antitheses are ironic in the sense that Richard hardly shares the pretensions of Edward's court, a court that we know, either from the *Henry VI* plays or, shortly, from Anne's lament over the corpse of Henry VI, does not represent a reconciliation of two warring factions but rather a temporary or apparent suppression of one faction by the other. This peacetime, then, and the sovereignty of the usurper Edward, can be thought of fundamentally not as the cessation of violence but as its institutionalization. In Richard's extended figure for the current situation, it is still "grim-visaged war," merely presenting a peaceful front, that has transferred its activities from the battlefield to the bedroom. To use the rhetorical terms introduced earlier, what Richard seems to appreciate is the nonproper or "improper" status of his brother's position. This position is congruent

with the rhetorical violence of naming, being constituted by the structurally analogous compound violence first of civil war—in which each side
sees the other as that which prevents itself from appearing proper, unique,
and authoritative—then of peace—in which the dream of the proper made
possible (and impossible) by war is rewritten by the "winning" side as the
ground and governing principle of national, political, and social identities.

    Abjuring that ground determined by Edward's usurpation (and the
position dictated for him in Edward's court), Richard ought logically to
extend his ironic insight to himself. A second antithesis—between the
erotic activities in terms of which Edward's peace is defined and Richard's
place within that schema—does make Richard's self-characterization doubly problematic.

> But I, that am not shaped for sportive tricks
> Nor made to court an amorous looking glass;
> I, that am rudely stamped, and want love's majesty
> To strut before a wanton ambling nymph.
>
>   (1.1.14–17)

Not only does the antithetical construction itself display each term's dependence upon the other but the first term of the antithesis, amorous
peace, has already been presented as highly unstable. At this point, however, the point where a subject, an "I," begins to be elaborated, Richard's
discourse parts company with rigor. The self that first emerges as the antithesis to the second term of a previous antithesis comes to appear instead
as itself the ground of these antitheses. In a long anacoluthon (the perfect
grammatical correlative for seduction, being a sentence or expression in
which there is a change of direction, an abandonment of one type of construction in favor of another) Richard translates his ironic, antithetically
constituted figure of the self into the unproblematic origin or source of his
speech and actions, locking himself into the sense of autonomous selfhood
that leads him to be such a poor legislator and poet in the end.

    The passage whose first four lines I just quoted continues:

> I, that am curtailed of this fair proportion
> Cheated of feature by dissembling Nature,
> Deformed, unfinished, sent before my time
> Into this breathing world scarce half made up,
> And that so lamely and unfashionable
> That dogs bark at me as I halt by them;

> Why, I, in this weak piping time of peace,
> Have no delight to pass away the time,
> Unless to spy my shadow in the sun
> And descant on mine own deformity.
>
> (1.1.18–27)

Suddenly, here, "peace" is peace and "I" am I; the constitutive negativity of Richard's self-image is skewed in the translation to become merely a negative (but otherwise stable, transparent) self-image. Like the narcissist that the reference to his shadow suggests that he is, Richard becomes attached to this *image* of what and where he is—an image first formulated, you recall, as an image of what and where he is not—at the expense of any apparent awareness or memory of the rhetorical operations that produced this illusory ground. He confounds the power of his demystifying insight into Edward's authority with a power that would generate the freedom of an authority of his own (a confusion that seduces many resistance groups, including feminists). In spirit he has already become a usurper—someone who holds a position without right and by force—not least in the sense that he now claims to be self-determining, a position that can be maintained only by doing both rhetorical and empirical violence to the figures and factors that constitute his position. "And therefore, since I cannot prove a lover," Richard concludes with logical illogic, "To entertain these fair well-spoken days, / I am determined to prove a villain / And hate the idle pleasures of these days" (1.1.28–31).

Richard, then, continues to deceive himself when he says at the close of the second scene, the seduction of Anne, that he cannot see in himself, as Anne seems to, a "proper" man. The powerfully seductive appeal of the narcissistic or rhetorical reflection by which Richard translates his analyses of others' positions and constructs his plots for their exploitation or extinction is precisely that it allows him to conceive of himself as a substantial being, a knowing and knowable "proper" subject, capable of autonomy and self-sovereignty. Anne is then delegated the unenviable task of sustaining and extending the business that Richard has begun in his soliloquy. She, for instance, can allow him to see reflected in her a self that is not deformed but proper in the sense of physically complete and sexually eligible. Anne's role, that is, will not prove to be determined in some simple cause and effect way by the sovereign subject Richard takes himself to be; on the contrary, it will be greatly determined by the insatiable need of such a "sovereign" subject to set up for itself new challenges to surmount in an ever-intensifying evasion of its own unraveling.

But distracting attention from how scene 2 breaks down the notion that Richard and Anne are two independent subjects, controversy over their interaction has focused on the much safer question of whether or not their dialogue is credible. Does it display Richard's brilliance and dramatic power that he can persuade Anne to marry him even though he has killed her husband and her father-in-law, even though he woos her over the corpse of her father-in-law, the murdered King Henry VI? Or is Anne a singularly weak woman? Or does the scene present an unplayable violation of dramatic and psychological probability, attributable, perhaps, to Shakespeare's immaturity as a playwright? None of these approaches will yield readings that account for the etiology of the appetites of a self-seducer like Richard or the particular vulnerability of Anne and Richard to each other. Those who argue that this scene is a brilliant display of Richard's talents simply reiterate Richard's own self-serving, long-winded, but unfounded assessment of his performance as a *tour de force* carried out in the face of every improbability:

> What! I that killed her husband and her father
> To take her in her heart's extremest hate,
> With curses in her mouth, tears in her eyes,
> The bleeding witness of my hatred by,
> Having God, her conscience, and these bars against me,
> And I no friends to back my suit at all
> But the plain devil and dissembling looks,
> And yet to win her, all the world to nothing!
>
> (1.2.230–37)

Conversely, but also similarly, those who find Anne weak or the scene improbable so thoroughly defend themselves against its shock effect that they see nothing to be investigated.

Thus commentators have generally not noted that it is Anne who first sets the terms for scene 2, nor have they said what those terms are. In her description of the dead Henry VI, we find her opposing signs of various kinds to more substantial realities that she takes to be transcendentally, genealogically, and even physiologically grounded:

> Poor key-cold figure of a holy king,
> Pale ashes of the house of Lancaster
> Thou bloodless remnant of that royal blood.
>
> (1.2.5–7)

The figures, that is, by which Anne has been defined, and continues to define herself when she identifies herself as "poor Anne, / Wife to thy Edward, to thy slaughtered son" (1.2.9–10), are posited, not as themselves figural or allegorical indicators of the rhetorical and empirical violence constitutive of political dominance (as Richard was able to see in instances other than his own) but as the literal embodiments of the authority they exercised. Though it might be seen that the War of the Roses would long since have radically disturbed, or displayed as disturbable, the status of names and titles associated with the houses of Lancaster and York, war can just as well, as I have mentioned, promise to each side the kind of stability of identity whose seductive appeal seems to govern the English court.

But Anne does not assume for herself quite the same kind of unproblematic position that she assumes for royal men. Implicit in her scheme of things is a kind of double focus or double bind whereby a woman's position and identity are thought of as derivative, and therefore in some sense representative, of a male position, while a woman is also supposed to possess the kind of autonomous subjectivity (akin to the subjectivity that we have watched Richard elaborate) that could ground distinctions like the ones Anne makes here between the figural and literal. The prophetic curse in Anne's opening speech, spoken, let it be noted, before Richard's entrance, displays the strange logic of her situation more obviously:

> If ever he have wife, let her be made
> More miserable by the life of him
> Than I am made by my young lord and thee [Henry VI].
> (1.2.26–28)

As much an anacoluthonist as Richard, she reasons that as her own unhappiness is an extension of the deaths of her husband and father-in-law, so the harm she wishes to Richard would be heightened and extended if his wife, should he ever have one, were to suffer on his account. This hypothetical wife (who will, of course, turn out to be Anne herself) would reflect her husband's condition, yet this reflection would also act somehow as a constituent of the condition it is supposed to reflect. Richard's role in the seduction of Anne is, thus, less self-initiated than it might at first appear. In a sense it is written for him, in Anne's discourse, before he ever approaches her. He need only respond to the double nature of her bereavement—her loss of her male points of reference and her role as a subjectivity that thinks of *itself* as authoritative. He can make her "amends," as he puts it at the end of scene 1, by repeatedly inviting her to see herself *reflected in him*, as immensely powerful. Whatever the fundamental incoherence and self-destructiveness of it, the position to which Anne is thus restored is consistent with (and might well seem even stronger than) the position out of which she has been cast.

It remains to be seen in greater detail how Anne's empirical seduction both evidences and screens from view Richard's and Anne's respective self-seductions, and, especially, how the image of male supremacy that Richard contrives to see reflected in Anne blinds him to the second major step on his course toward disaster. Two examples, one from the beginning of the dialogue and one from near the end, will have to suffice here to suggest in outline the remarkable transaction carried out in this complex, highly nuanced exchange. A moment after Richard has terrorized the pall-bearers and been defied by Anne, he hails her as someone who has a more positive, powerful part to play than that of bereaved and beleaguered widow: "Sweet saint, for charity, be not so curst" (1.2.49), he intervenes unexpectedly. By doing so, he pays her the compliment of adopting her constellation of terms—she has just called him a devil and a "dreadful minister of hell" (1.2.46)—and names her in a way that lends the authority of virtue to her claims and curses —an authority that she evidently accepts in her lengthy, eloquently vituperative response to Richard's address. Her acceptance of his use of her terms, as well as his appropriation of her terms, however, sets up a paradoxical dependency. In order for Anne to remain the author, the creator, of the terms she is using and to retain her sense that hers is the definitive description of the situation—in order to be a speaker at all, really—she will have to remain in conversation with Richard, as in fact she does—their extensive repartee serving to consolidate this dependence. On the other hand, Richard's encouragement of Anne's sense of her own power over herself and Richard—which reaches its apotheosis when Richard offers her his sword and encourages her to kill him—encourages Richard, too, to think of himself as author and director of the situation, making him, in turn, paradoxically dependent upon Anne's continuing sense of authorship.

Anne, if the other female characters in the tetralogy are any indication, has no habitual or socially available alternative. These are the conditions, we can surmise, under which she would always have operated, and, on balance, Richard seems to offer her more rather than less self-determination. But how does Richard manage to have Anne serve as a testimonial to his manipulative talents and still recuperate her as a powerful, power-giving figure? His failure (and Anne's) to understand that both figures are shadowy projections of his own rhetorical blindness is enacted in their closing exchange where Anne reluctantly accepts Richard's ring. Anne, mistakenly, asserts, "To take is not to give" (1.2.203–4), to which Richard cynically, but with inadvertent accuracy, responds:

> Look how my ring encompasseth thy finger,
> Even so thy breast encloseth my poor heart.
> Wear both of them, for both of them are thine.
>   (1.2.230–32)

Anne, that is, reflecting her insistence upon an illusory autonomy, tries to take the ring and run, to extricate herself from the conversation with her sense of her separateness from Richard intact. In the act of doing so, however, she gives, or seems to give, Richard exactly what he wants, namely that very separateness. It is *precisely* the moment at which Anne reasserts her autonomy that is seized upon by Richard in order to see reflected in her an objective, external indicator of his power. (Later, in an effort to repeat and eternalize this maneuver, he will arrange to make the appearance of her autonomy permanent by having her murdered.) His unselfconscious use of a Petrarchan conceit to do so, however, labels him as at once a show-off and a dupe. Ironically a much better index of his situation than his supposed success with Anne, the discourse he employs as a sign of his literary and amorous sophistication, remains, in an important sense, unreadable to him. Because of his unironic assumption of mastery *over* his own (and Petrarch's) discourse, he remains utterly blind to what it has to say about the futility of his logic.

What Richard's words display, without necessarily expressing, might be put this way: If Anne's acceptance of his ring validates Richard's capacity to determine what will signify what to whom, then the "heart" or being of Richard, itself a product of signification, could be said to be "enclosed" within—in the sense of limited by—Anne's acceptance. It follows that Richard retains no autonomous self but could be described as a kind of ornament, set off to great advantage as presented or worn by Anne. Anne's own status is, of course, neither more nor less problematic than Richard's, as is suggested by the contorted image of her wearing the heart that her breast also encloses. That Richard can offer and Anne can accept these words without either of them becoming alive to these implications then underscores one further aspect of their situation—namely, that because of their kindred, though asymmetrical, attachments to rhetorically impossible ideals of selfhood, both Richard and Anne cut themselves off from what discourse might have to tell them. The final irony is, of course, that the abstraction of the self from language that they seek is exactly that which, in a sense not consciously intended, they also find.

III

Some repercussions of my project of Richard's misappropriation of language are by now obvious. If either deconstruction or feminism were to triumph over the other, I would have to count it a loss for both. To criticize one discourse at the expense of the other would not prove that the first is better, nor must we try to make them consistent with each other in order to be rigorous. Indeed such projects can make sense only within the kind of totalizing discourse with which I have been taking issue. If I have not seen a way simply and directly to extricate Anne from her predicament, owing to my insistence upon analyzing her situation rhetorically rather than empirically, neither have I, I hope, encouraged a utopian feminism that would be compatible with other, nonwoman-centered, utopian dreams—of which, after all, Richard's is one.

Savage Play in *Richard III*

C. L. Barber and Richard P. Wheeler

Instead of two brothers indistinguishable, Richard III's manifesto is "I have no brother, I am like no brother" (*3 Henry VI*, 5.6.80). Richard's brilliant playing-within-the-play is often farcical, but savage motivation for it is emphatically explicit. So are the consequences—and dread of them. Instead of the final maternal blessing of *The Comedy of Errors*, we have the outraged and outrageous curses of Margaret and the chorus of bereft maternal figures, including Richard's mother, who finally also curses him. The tragical history is the obverse of the comedy in its handling of the ties between brother and brother, son and mother. In his exploration of fratricidal violence and mother-son structures of fear and hate, Shakespeare goes far down, or far back, in dramatic understanding of motives growing from the family constellation, with more explicit reference to infancy and childhood than we get in any other play. He licenses theatrical aggression in a way that is new for him, and at the same time builds a complex formal structure to contain it. His extrapolation of family motives, far beyond suggestions in his sources, skillfully makes these motives part of the social pathology, though . . . his dramatization of the political resolution lacks the cogency of the play's dreadful logic of family violence.

"INDUCTIONS DANGEROUS"

As games may do in life when one of the players breaks the social compact on which playfulness depends, the games Richard plays move be-

From *The Whole Journey: Shakespeare's Power of Development*. © 1986 by the Regents of the University of California. University of California Press, 1986.

yond play to actual hurting. A player who keeps doing this is soon likely to be isolated—unless the whole gang joins in and makes the game into hurting, as with street gangs. Richard has been brought up in such a gang, the house of York in the contention of the two noble houses of York and Lancaster. The broad-gauged chronicle history of the Henry VI plays shifts to a highly formalized drama built around a single protagonist as Richard decides to go it alone after being the most savage partisan of a savage lot.

Already in the middle of *3 Henry VI* he announces his covert intentions in a long self-revelatory soliloquy; the scenario and the character to animate it are presented with unprecedented explicitness. The shift to solitary villainy takes place after Richard kills sainted King Henry in the last act. First he speaks as a partisan: "What? will the aspiring blood of Lancaster / Sink in the ground? I thought it would have mounted" (5.6.61–62). Then he responds to Henry's execrations about his loathsome birth, legs forward, body hunched, his teeth already in:

> And so I was, which plainly signified
> That I should snarl, and bite, and play the dog.
> Then since the heavens have shap'd my body so,
> Let hell make crook'd my mind to answer it.
> I have no brother, I am like no brother;
> And this word "love," which greybeards call divine,
> Be resident in men like one another,
> And not in me: I am myself alone.
> Clarence, beware! thou keep'st me from the light.
>
> (ll. 76–84)

"I am myself alone"—and yet Richard is gamesome. He can play, with a zest realized here for the first time, because in fact he is not alone: he has the theater audience, whom he now addresses, to play with—"Had I not reason, *think ye*, to make haste" (l. 72). A playful stage villain depends on the fact that "men like one another" are similar, not only in their susceptibility to "this word 'love' " but also to the pleasure of rejecting social and moral restraints.

Villainous wit, and hypocrisy that we can see through as it pays a specious tribute to virtue, both involve the tendentious manipulation of a verbal and social surface. As *Richard III* begins the audience is elaborately cued to see through to what is under Richard's hypocrisy:

> Plots have I laid, inductions dangerous, . . .
> And if King Edward be as true and just

> As I am subtle, false, and treacherous,
> This day should Clarence closely be mew'd up
> About a prophecy which says that G
> Of Edward's heirs the murtherer shall be.
>
> Dive, thoughts, down to my soul, here Clarence comes!
> *Enter Clarence, guarded, and Brakenbury, [Lieutenant of the Tower].*
> Brother, good day. What means this armed guard
> That waits upon your Grace?
> CLARENCE: His Majesty,
> Tend'ring my person's safety, hath appointed
> This conduct to convey me to the Tower.
> RICHARD: Upon what cause?
> CLARENCE: Because my name is George.
> RICHARD: Alack, my lord, that fault is none of yours;
> He should for that commit your godfathers.
>
>   (1.1.32,36–48)

Richard takes up Clarence's bitter irony about his name and winds the fancy around to allude to the butt of malmsey wine in which Clarence is to be drowned, a circumstance so familiar from the chronicles that many first-time auditors would be able to share his private joke: "O, belike his Majesty hath some intent / That you should be new christ'ned in the Tower" (ll. 49–50). Then comes a characteristic shift into his plausible "plain man" (1.3.51) vein to express brotherly concern—"But what's the matter, Clarence, may I know?" (1.1.51)—which Clarence takes at face value.

After his brother has retailed the king's superstitious fears of the letter G, Richard displaces the blame to Edward's common-born queen, with scorn that speaks solidarity with his royal brother:

> Why, this it is, when men are rul'd by women:
> 'Tis not the King that sends you to the Tower;
> My Lady Grey his wife, Clarence, 'tis she
> That tempers him to this extremity. . . . .
> We are not safe, Clarence, we are not safe.
>
>   (1.1.62–65,70)

Richard is virtuoso with displacement, representation through the opposite, allusion, all the "wit mechanisms" that Freud saw to be active also in the dream work and that transform latent content into the manifest dream.

His wit gives the play the quality of a bad dream, one where for the audience the latent content has been made manifest, in contrast to *The Comedy of Errors*.

Richard is expert, indeed inspired, in the kind of thinking that moves through the corporeality of a word from one of its senses to another, as when Rivers takes up Queen Elizabeth's protest that she has been falsely accused:

> RICHARD: You may deny that you were not the mean
>   Of my Lord Hastings' late imprisonment.
> RIVERS: She may, my lord, for—
> RICHARD: She may, Lord Rivers! Why, who knows not so?
>   She may do more, sir, than denying that:
>   She may help you to many fair preferments,
>   And then deny her aiding hand therein
>   And lay those honors on your high desert.
>   What may she not, she may, ay, marry, may she.
> RIVERS: What, marry, may she?
> RICHARD: What, marry, may she! Marry with a king,
>   A bachelor, and a handsome stripling too:
>   Iwis your grandam had a worser match.
>
> (1.3.89–101)

A manic energy animates such aggressive wit, like the manic physical energy with which an accomplished actor can move Richard's deformed body. Richard's artful management of the social surface is conducted with wonderful plausibility—"We are not safe, Clarence, we are not safe." We in the audience can hear: "You are not safe, Clarence, you are not safe." The relation between the two levels is expressed spatially in "Dive, thoughts, down to my soul, here Clarence comes!"

The menace complicates or interrupts simple amusement. That people in the play take Richard's hypocrisy at face value often depends as much on a conventional theatrical compact as does our accepting that no one on stage in *The Comedy of Errors* should realize he is dealing with identical twins. One of the formal conventions Shakespeare is adapting is explicit in "Thus, like the formal Vice, Iniquity, / I moralize two meanings in one word" (3.1.82–83). The Vice's role gives scope for representation through the opposite in the guise of pious charades:

> Poor Clarence did forsake his father, Warwick,
> Ay, and forswore himself—which Jesu pardon!—. . .

> To fight on Edward's party for the crown,
> And for his meed, poor lord, he is mewed up.
> I would to God my heart were flint, like Edward's,
> Or Edward's soft and pitiful, like mine:
> I am too childish-foolish for this world.
>
> (1.3.134–35, 137–41)

We are invited to hoot at such transparent flummery. Or Richard himself breaks up the social surface. After the reconciliation the dying King Edward thinks he has brought about, his poor queen wants to believe in it:

> My sovereign lord, I do beseech your Highness
> To take our brother Clarence to your grace.
> RICHARD: Why, madam, have I off'red love for this,
> To be so flouted in this royal presence?
> Who knows not that the gentle Duke is dead?
>
> *They all start.*
> (2.1.76–80)

Richard repeatedly disrupts scenes in this way. Besides double entendres and asides, he uses abrupt, naked ruthlessness, the "sudden stab of rancor" (3.2.87).

> BUCKINGHAM: Now, my lord, what shall we do if we perceive
> Lord Hastings will not yield to our complots?
> RICHARD: Chop off his head!
>
> (3.1.191–93)

Richard here is Punch throwing the troublesome baby out the window, simplifying the problem of government as Punch simplifies the problem of child care. We cannot resist something like glee at such a moment, with a laugh close to a gasp.

The difference from Punch of course is that the serious consequences of this savage farce are kept before us. In the scene that immediately follows, we are caught up in anxiety for Hastings as he ignores the warning of Stanley's ominous dream that "the boar had rased off his helm" (3.2.11). Our concern is then complicated by Hastings's own cruelty about the sudden execution of the queen's kindred. Richard's strategy of playing the old nobility off against the new, explicitly described in the sources, works as Catesby brings the news that the Queen's kindred are to die. The aristocrat is as ruthless in his bland way as the future usurper, even though he will not go along with usurpation:

HASTINGS: Well, Catesby, ere a fortnight make me older,
    I'll send some packing that yet think not on't.
CATESBY: 'Tis a vile thing to die, my gracious lord,
    When men are unprepar'd and look not for it.
HASTINGS: O monstrous, monstrous! and so falls it out
    With Rivers, Vaughan, Grey; and so 'twill do
    With some men else, that think themselves as safe
    As thou and I, who (as thou know'st) are dear
    To princely Richard and to Buckingham.
CATESBY: The princes both make high account of you—
    [*Aside.*] For they account his head upon the bridge.
                             (3.2.60–70)

The play combines the appeals of stage villainy with clear-eyed presentation of a whole complex world of court intrigue, its bad faith and
callous cruelty. After pious protestation about the sanctity of sanctuary,
the archbishop complies in getting the child duke of York out of sanctuary. The lord mayor connives. Shakespeare underlines how moral weakness and failure of nerve contribute to the political maneuvers recorded in
Sir Thomas More's *History of Richard III* as transcribed in the chronicles.
Our flesh creeps as we watch victims being ensnared in Richard's web, especially with Clarence and the little princes. Yet at the same time, in the
first three acts, until the crown is won the villain fascinates us and even
delights us. Richard is the first of the line of figures, all in one way or
another either alienated or outsiders, whom Shakespeare endows with
some of his own dramatic powers, most notably Falstaff, Hamlet, and
Iago. He is also Shakespeare's first great exploitation of theatrical aggression, the turning of acting into action, fundamental to Marlowe's and
Kyd's radically disruptive use of the new dramatic medium. Richard's alliance with the audience is similar in some ways to Tamburlaine's, in that
it works to free aggressive energies from conscience.

Yet unlike *Tamburlaine, Richard III* is emphatically designed to contain
the theatrical aggression within a larger pattern. Richard has to do his savage playing within the net of retributory curses initiated by Margaret; he
is their agent, only finally to be subject to them himself. His disruptive
energy is also contained by being understood, both as the product of the
great family feud Shakespeare has dramatized and as an individual psychology shaped by his physical deformity and the rejection it comes to embody.

The contrast with Marlowe's radical theatrical aggression is clearest in
The Jew of Malta. Marlowe's Punch-like figure, with his enormous "*Hal-*

cions bill," is an alienated alien; Shakespeare's alienated villain is at the very center of established society. Barabas is as ruthless as Richard in disposing of family ties, but he has only one, to his daughter—no mother or father or childhood. Both are self-proclaimed Machiavels, and both bring out and show up the venal ruthlessness beneath moral hypocrisy, of people around them, enlisting us in the enterprise. But Marlowe's savage farce exhibits his hero as the epitome of motives animating the *whole* society; there is nothing but aggressive greed and hypocritical cover: "Welcome, great *Bashaws,* how fares *Callymath,* / What wind drives you thus into *Malta* rhode?" The answer summarizes the play's whole society: "The wind that bloweth all the world besides, / Desire of gold" (ll. 1420–24). One must except poor Abigail's love for Mathias, but it is really there to provide the occasion for Barabas to turn her lover and his rival into mutually destructive puppets: "O brauely fought, and yet they thrust not home. / Now *Lodowicke,* now *Mathias,* so; / So now they haue shew'd themselues to be tall fellowes" (ll. 1186–88). By contrast with the vitality of this, Abigail's grief is perfunctorily dealt with as she leaves for the convent—and her share of the poisoned pot of porridge. The radical perspective and terse scorn of Marlowe's play depend on a devastating rejection of social values, including their roots in relationship to the feminine, utterly different from Shakespeare's embrace of the whole society even as he exhibits it being subverted. Like Richard, Barabas makes an appeal to honesty about ruthlessness: "As good dissemble that thou neuer mean'st / As first mean truth and then dissemble it" (ll. 528–29). But Marlowe engages us in seeing through morality. The whole construction in *The Jew of Malta,* like the hero, forces radical awareness on us. As the governor ends the play with a blatantly conventional concluding couplet, there can be nothing but a jeering response: "So march away, and let due praise be giuen / Neither to Fate nor Fortune, but to Heauen" (ll. 2409–10).

"And Am I Then a Man to Be Belov'd?"

In presenting given historical events in *Richard III*, Shakespeare molds them and supplements them in ways characteristic of the shaping influence of his sensibility in his early works. Along with the incarnation of specifically theatrical power in Richard, the most striking thing is the way the dramatist defines Richard in domestic and sexual terms, pitting his power against women as well as a brother. There are suggestions for some of this, as we shall see, in the chronicles; but most of it is Shakespeare's adaptation or purely fictive extrapolation. The murder of Clarence, which in the play is contemporary with King Edward's final illness and is all Richard's doing, in fact occurred years earlier and by Edward's orders. There is only a suggestion in the chronicles that Richard's hostility contributed to the king's action. Queen Margaret, Henry VI's widow, had died in France well before King Edward's death. Our familiarity with the play as it stands can obscure the drastic originality of Shakespeare's bringing her back to serve as maleficent chorus and Richard's principal emotional antagonist—a figure almost equal to him in dramatic and poetic energy.

If one regards *Richard III* as the finale of the Henry VI plays, Margaret's role is less surprising than it would otherwise be, not only because she serves so beautifully as a channel through which that past is brought to bear on the present, but because on a deeper level she continues the series of overweening or overpowering women in those plays, being herself their most extreme instance. Until Shakespeare arrives at his conception of Richard, none of the men can match these women, with one entirely invented exception—Talbot's turning the tables on the Countess of Auvergne. Joan de Pucelle takes over the Dauphin, after defeating him in a trial of strength; even Talbot cannot overcome her in single combat! Only after her fiends melodramatically forsake her is the captured witch led in, spitting curses—and immediately we see Suffolk bewitched by the beauty of his captive, Margaret of Navarre. His ambiguously motivated project of marrying her to weak King Henry is set up before we see Joan exposed as a vainglorious upstart. Joan denies her own father and is proved to be a mere woman after all, sexually promiscuous and ready to plead "the fruit within my womb" (*1 Henry VI*, 5.4.63) in a vain effort to avoid the stake. Male superiority is restored with York's taunt, "Why, here's a girl! I think she knows not well / (There were so many) whom she may accuse"(5.4.80–81). But the final scene shows King Henry consenting to the marriage with the woman who is to dominate him in the two following plays, becoming in time the murderous virago with a "tiger's heart wrapp'd in a woman's hide" (*3 Henry VI*, 1.4.137). As her role develops we also watch the Lord Protector, the Good Duke Humphrey, prove helpless to cope with his overweening wife; then he is murdered, partly in consequence, by the queen and Suffolk's faction.

Much of this was taken over from Shakespeare's chronicle sources, if often rearranged, and of course focused on selected persons and moments. Shakespeare shapes his materials in the direction of the domestic patterns here described, but he does so in the course of pioneering the dramatization of history. He is interested in the whole life of England, his England, as Marlowe's alienated genius never was, even when he too pioneered the use of English historical materials in *Edward II*. The focus in *1 Henry VI* is on patriotic heroics and lament as Henry V's conquests in France are lost despite Talbot's heroism. The dramatization of Joan's power is balanced by chauvinistic celebration of the male bond of battle. The emotional climax is the death of Talbot with his dead son in his arms, after the son has refused to escape the encircling French and has proved his fledgling honor. When one sees the play performed one realizes how effectively the company were serving interests now catered to by popular films of patriotic violence. Nashe's familiar account of Talbot's "bones newe embalmed with teares of ten thousand spectators at least" (*Pierce Penilesse,* 1592) makes vivid its Elizabethan public appeal. Such battle heroics are never dropped from Shakespeare's histories, which all reach climax in them, often with emotional atonements of dying heroes: at Agincourt in *Henry V,* Suffolk and York are together lovingly "espous'd to death" (4.6.26). But even in *Henry VI: Part 1* vital public issues of authority and loyalty, faction and subversion, are brought out, and these come into clearer and clearer focus in *Part 2* and *Part 3.* The murder of good Duke Humphrey opens the way for the Wars of the Roses, with the telling study of the social consequences of King Henry's weakness despite his spirituality. The exemplary function of history becomes particularly prominent in the last play, in the choric scene during the battle of Towton where King Henry's meditations on the happy life of the homely swain are interrupted by "a Son that hath kill'd his father," and "a Father that hath kill'd his son" (2.5).

The Henry VI plays are conducted so as to exhibit "what mischiefe hath insurged in realmes by intestine devision," with relatively little aggressive use of the theatrical medium as such. There is a moment of almost egregious imitation of Marlowe in *Part 2* as York returns to England with "his army of Irish" (s.d.):

> From Ireland thus comes York to claim his right,
> And pluck the crown from feeble Henry's head.
> Ring bells, aloud, burn bonfires clear and bright
> To entertain great England's lawful king!
> Ah, *sancta majestas!* who would not buy thee dear?
> Let them obey that knows not how to rule;
> This hand was made to handle nought but gold.
>
> (*2 Henry VI*, 5.1.1–7)

But this echo of Tamburlaine on heaven entertaining Zenocrate is not typical, and its effect on the audience cannot be mesmeric: too much else is in action. So too with Richard's momentary rise into Marlowe's idiom as he urges his father, York, to break his covenant:

> How sweet a thing it is to wear a crown,
> Within whose circuit is Elysium
> And all that poets feign of bliss and joy.
>
> (*3 Henry VI*, 1.2.29–31)

The whole pattern by which "Measure for measure must be answered" (*3 Henry VI*, 2.6.54) is much too strongly realized to be taken over by any such one-way visions of omnipotence. Richard's talk of Elysium persuades his father to make the fatal sortie from Sandal Castle. It will put him, captive, at Margaret's mercy:

> Where are your mess of sons to back you now,
> The wanton Edward, and the lusty George?
> And where's that valiant crook-back prodigy,
> Dicky, your boy, that with his grumbling voice
> Was wont to cheer his dad in mutinies?
> Or with the rest, where is your darling, Rutland?
> Look, York, I stain'd this napkin with [his] blood.
>
> (*3 Henry VI*, 1.4.73–79)

—and so on to the paper crown and her joining in stabbing York to death. (In the chronicles his head is brought to her in the camp.)

So long as his strong father is alive, Richard's violence is dedicated to his support. The sudden new development of theatrical power in his role accords with his decision to seek the crown for himself. The long soliloquy that first announces Richard's ruthless ambition comes immediately after his brother has used newly acquired royal power to make Lady Grey his wife. In the historical sources the onset of Richard's determination to usurp the crown did not become manifest until years later. There is a dynamic coherence, however, in Shakespeare's putting it soon after the loss of the father who has focused the sons' loyalty and sanctioned their aggression against others—and immediately after the older brother's emphatically sexual commitment to marriage.

Taunts by Richard and Clarence about Edward's sexual appetite precede Richard's account of his own sexual unfitness. Edward has made Lady Grey's silence do for her consent: "Widow, go you along. Lords, use her honorably."

> Ay, Edward will use women honorably.
> Would he were wasted, marrow, bones, and all,
> That from his loins no hopeful branch may spring,
> To cross me from the golden time I look for!
>
> (*3 Henry VI*, 3.2.123–27)

Richard's "soul's desire" blocked not only by "lustful Edward's title" but by another older brother and the "unlooked for issue of their bodies," he pauses momentarily to consider the alternative: "What other pleasure can the world afford?" He dismisses as "miserable" and "unlikely" the prospect of narcissistically rewarding sexual conquest with his stunning account of the history and implications of his deformity:

> Why, love forswore me in my mother's womb;
> And for I should not deal in her soft laws,
> She did corrupt frail nature with some bribe,
> To shrink mine arm up like a wither'd shrub,
> To make an envious mountain on my back,
> Where sits deformity to mock my body;
> To shape my legs of an unequal size,
> To disproportion me in every part,
> Like to a chaos, or an unlick'd bear-whelp
> That carries no impression like the dam.
>
> (ll. 153–62)

Finding himself no "man to be belov'd," Richard returns to his overriding desire:

> Then since this earth affords no joy to me
> But to command, to check, to o'erbear such
> As are of better person than myself,
> I'll make my heaven to dream upon the crown.
>
> (ll. 165–68)

Richard's deformity and the rumor about his unnatural birth were in the chronicles. But sexual frustration as a consequence, and so the motive for compensatory villainy, is entirely from Shakespeare. The opening soliloquy of *Richard III* is so familiar that it is easy to overlook the fact that there is no historical basis for its neat antithesis:

> And therefore, since I cannot prove a lover
> To entertain these fair well-spoken days,
> I am determined to prove a villain
> And hate the idle pleasures of these days.
>
> (1.1.28–31)

The chronicles do contain a circumstantial narrative of Richard's astonishing outburst about being bewitched, in the council meeting over the coronation, at which he turned on Hastings and sprang his coup d'etat. In Edward Hall's transcription of Thomas More, Richard arrives late because "he had been a sleper that daye." As in the play, he sends the Bishop of

Ely to fetch strawberries, then leaves the chamber. He returns "all chaunged with a sowre angry countenaunce knittyng the browes, frowynng and fretyng and gnawyng on his lips" as the dismayed lords marvel at "what thyng should hym ayle." Richard sits silent for a time, then asks: "What were they worthy to have that compasse and ymagine the destrucion of me beyng so neare of bloud to the kyng & protectour of this his royall realme: At which question, all the lordes sate sore astonyed, musyng muche by whom the question should be ment, of which every man knew him self clere." Hastings answers that "they were worthy to be punished as heynous traytors," and when the others agree, Richard accuses "yonder sorceres my brothers wife and other with her, menying the quene. At these woordes many of the lordes were sore abashed which favoured her," though Hastings's only regret is that "he was not afore made of counsail of this matter":

> Then sayed the protectour in what wyse that sorceresse and
> other of her counsayle, as Shores wyfe with her affinitie have
> by their sorcery and witchecrafte this wasted my body, and
> therwith plucked up his doublet sleve to his elbowe on hys left
> arme, where he shewed a weryshe wythered arme & smalle as
> it was never other.

More then describes the misgivings Richard's accusation produces in "every mannes mynde, . . . well perceyvyng that this matter was but a quarell," for the queen was "too wyse to go about any such folye," and would in any case scarcely have turned to Shore's wife, "whom of all women she most hated as that concubine whom the kyng her husband most loved." "Also, there was no manne there but knewe that hys arme was ever such sith the day of his birth."

Hastings, whose "hart somewhat grudged to have her whom he loved so highly accused, . . . aunswered and sayed, certaynly my lorde, yf they have so done, they be worthy of heynous punishement." In More's account, the particular vehemence against Hastings is compounded by the arrest of the other lords by armed men summoned by Richard's signal:

> What quod the protectour, thou servest me I wene with yf and
> with and, I tell the they have done it, and that wyll I make
> good on thy bodye, traytour. And therwith (as in a great an-
> ger) he clapped hys fyste on the borde a great rappe, at whiche
> token geven, one cried treason without the chamber, and there-
> with a doore clapped, and in came rushyng men in harneyes as

many as the chamber could hold. And anone the protectoure sayed to the lorde Hastynges, I arrest thee traytoure, what me my lorde quod he: yea thee traytoure quod the protectour. And one let flye at the lorde Stanley, which shroncke at the stroacke and fell under the table, or els hys head had bene cleft to the teth, for as shortly as he shrancke, yet ranne the bloud aboute hys eares. Then was the Archebishop of Yorke and the doctour Morton bishopp of Ely & the lorde Stanley taken and divers other whiche were bestowed in dyvers chambers, save the lorde Hastynges (whom the protectour commaunded to spede and shryve him apace) for by sainct Poule (quod he) I wyll not dyne tyll I se thy head off.

The event is unforgettable as Shakespeare compresses it into a coup de theatre:

> Look how I am bewitch'd; behold, mine arm
> Is like a blasted sapling, wither'd up;
> And this is Edward's wife, that monstrous witch,
> Consorted with that harlot, strumpet Shore,
> That by their witchcraft thus have marked me.
> HASTINGS: If they have done this deed, my noble lord—
> RICHARD: If? Thou protector of this damned strumpet,
> Talk'st thou to me of "ifs"? Thou art a traitor.
> Off with his head! Now by Saint Paul I swear
> I will not dine until I see the same.
>
> (3.4.68–77)

It is a good corrective for a venture such as mine that this strange behavior of Richard is not invented by Shakespeare, but is in his source. Indeed something like the scene may actually have occurred; it seems scarcely possible that "doctour Morton bishopp of Ely," who is recorded as present and who was More's source, can have made up something so bizarre from whole cloth. Life can be as strange as art! The historical Richard may well have externalized his suffering over his deformity by accusations of witchcraft. To eliminate Hastings was part of the practical strategy of the coup—recorded in the sources at length, with emphasis on Hastings's ignoring of portents. But no practical motive can account for doing it through accusations of witchcraft against Richard's brother's wife and his former mistress, least likely of allies, as More's account notes. A projection which everyone can see through conveys a sense of injury by a woman or women who have "wasted my body." Jealous rage at the sexuality of more fortunate men finds a present object in Hastings, who is enjoying the hand-me-down mistress. "I wyll not dyne tyll I se thy head off" seems to fit, as does "make good on thy bodye," with a sense of deprivation that seeks resolution by eliminating a sexually competent and satisfied man.

Shakespeare's remarkable elaboration of Richard's relationship to women is extrapolated from this account, along with the rumors reported about his birth. At the same time it carries on the subject of overpowering women, which has occupied so much of the three earlier histories. There is a striking similarity, almost uncanny, between the council scene in the historical source of *Richard III* and the entirely invented scene between Talbot and the Countess of Auvergne near the beginning of the *Henry VI* series. The Countess tries to entrap the martial hero by luring him to dinner. Talbot takes the precaution of secretly infiltrating his soldiers into her castle. When he appears, alone, she mocks him; having expected a "second Hector," she claims to find him instead

> a child, a silly dwarf!
> It cannot be this weak and writhled shrimp
> Should strike such terror to his enemies.
>   (*1 Henry VI*, 2.3.20, 20–24)

She thinks she has closed the trap:

> COUNTESS: Long time thy shadow hath been thrall to me,
>   For in my gallery thy picture hangs;
>   But now thy substance shall endure the like, . . .
> TALBOT: I laugh to see your ladyship so fond
>   To think that you have ought but Talbot's shadow
>   Whereon to practice your severity. . . .
>   No, no, I am but shadow of myself.
>   You are deceiv'd, my substance is not here; . . .
>   *Winds his horn. Drums strike up; a peal of ordnance.*
>   *Enter soldiers.*
>   How say you, madam? Are you now persuaded
>   That Talbot is but shadow of himself?
>   There are his substance, sinews, arms, and strength.
>   (ll. 36–38, 45–47, 50–51, 61–63)

Here the disabling body imagery is cast upon the man, not as a spell but in scorn, by a woman who "compasses and imagines" his destruction, and who would "chain these arms and legs of thine" (l. 39). But she is baffled when he summons military force—much as in More's account of Richard with the council, where "in came rushyng men in harneyes as many as the chamber could hold." It may be mere coincidence, but the countess's picturesque phrase, "weak and writhled [withered] shrimp" fits with More's description of the "weryshe wythered arme and small" that Richard displays as proof of his being bewitched. It seems possible that Shakespeare, in designing this scene early in his sequence of histories, shaped it, consciously or unconsciously, from recollection of reading the account of Richard's coup in the chronicle. Be that as it may, what is manifest is that he invents an episode where a virtuous hero, dedicated to his country's service, turns the tables on a scheming, scornfully disabling woman, proving he is no "child" or "silly dwarf." Talbot's mastery is clinched when he chivalrously forgoes retaliation: "Be not dismay'd, fair lady, . . . / What you have done hath not offended me; / Nor other satisfaction do I crave"—but the wine and cates of the original dinner, "For soldiers' stomachs always serve them well" (ll. 73, 76–77, 80). He does not require her head before he dines! She does not have a "head" in the subliminal sense that is present as Richard takes vengeance on Hastings's sexuality along with his political intransigence. It is enough for Talbot's assertion of his manhood to use his male solidarity in war to force the French amazon back to her woman's role of providing food.

Talbot confidently relies on his troops to evade the snare set for him by the countess; Richard isolates himself from his own astonished council with the charge that Mistress Grey has ensnared him with her witchcraft. Set beside each other, these two scenes highlight both similarities and differences in the dramatic and psychological circumstances of the two plays. Beneath the male bonding in chivalric aggression of the earlier play, there is the potential of naked brother-to-brother aggression, which Shakespeare dramatizes as the fruit of the civil strife that undoes Talbot's achievements. Richard, instead of having command of chivalric and patriotic male solidarity to baffle threatening women felt as "strangers," must try to cope with those women who are closest to a child—or "the child in the man." Male solidarity in war and more generally in patriarchal institutions can serve as defense—one Richard does not have—against the child in the man. There is a sense in which Richard, trapped in his body and the fixation on rejection by women it symbolizes, is indeed "too childish-foolish for this world" (*Richard III*, 1.3.141). His violent pursuit of the crown seeks something like infantile omnipotence—and is ultimately foolish. But moment by moment, through his wit and his ruthlessness, he has tastes of such uncircumscribable power. His special role as a stage villain, by its alliance with the audience, also has power as an incarnation of plot; he shares with us a superior awareness of what will happen, which the other characters do not have.

Talbot also shares his plot with us as he whispers directions to a captain. But he is the very opposite of the lone stage villain. He turns the tables by his *social* role, emphasizing that he has power only through others: "I am but shadow of myself." Sigurd Burckhardt, in *Shakespearean Meanings,* uses that line as title of a chapter in which he suggests that we can see Talbot's expression of his relationship to his soldiers as a type of Shakespeare's relation to his dramatis personae. His actors are his "substance, sinews, arms, and strength" as the young dramatist takes over full control, "the only Shake-scene," after working on individual scenes in collaboration with more established playwrights. In developing this construction, Burckhardt emphasizes that the scene is entirely invented, and that Talbot is not in character with his role of chivalric derring-do everywhere else: "His strength lies precisely in his 'negative capability,' his having learned the secret of self-effacement, of assertion only through the larger design." Whether or not Burckhardt's equation of Talbot with Shakespeare was conscious for the author, it can stand for Shakespeare's relationship to his drama in the Henry VI plays. A very different relationship obtains when in *Richard III* he endows the isolated and obsessed king of the chronicles with his own verbal and dramatic powers. An explosion of creative energy accompanies the dramatization of the release of violent libidinal energy.

Chronology

1564	William Shakespeare born at Stratford-on-Avon to John Shakespeare, a butcher, and Mary Arden. He is baptized on April 26.
1582	Marries Anne Hathaway in November.
1583	Daughter Susanna born, baptized on May 26.
1585	Twins Hamnet and Judith born, baptized on February 2.
1588–90	Sometime during these years, Shakespeare goes to London, without family. First plays performed in London.
1590–92	*The Comedy of Errors*, the three parts of *Henry VI*.
1593–94	Publication of *Venus and Adonis* and *The Rape of Lucrece*, both dedicated to the earl of Southampton. Shakespeare becomes a sharer in the Lord Chamberlain's company of actors. *The Taming of the Shrew*, *The Two Gentlemen of Verona*, *Richard III*, *Titus Andronicus*.
1595–97	*Romeo and Juliet*, *Richard II*, *King John*, *A Midsummer Night's Dream*, *Love's Labor's Lost*.
1596	Son Hamnet dies. Grant of arms to Shakespeare's father.
1597	*The Merchant of Venice*, *Henry IV, Part 1*. Purchases New Place in Stratford.
1598–1600	*Henry IV, Part 2*, *As You Like It*, *Much Ado about Nothing*, *Twelfth Night*, *The Merry Wives of Windsor*, *Henry V*, and *Julius Caesar*. Moves his company to the new Globe Theatre.
1601	*Hamlet*. Shakespeare's father dies, buried on September 8.
1601–2	*Troilus and Cressida*.
1603	Death of Queen Elizabeth; James VI of Scotland becomes James I of England; Shakespeare's company becomes the King's Men.
1603–4	*All's Well That Ends Well*, *Measure for Measure*, *Othello*.

1605–6	*King Lear, Macbeth.*
1607	Marriage of daughter Susanna on June 5.
1607–8	*Timon of Athens, Antony and Cleopatra, Pericles, Coriolanus.*
1608	Shakespeare's mother dies, buried on September 9.
1609	*Cymbeline*, publication of sonnets. Shakespeare's company purchases Blackfriars Theatre.
1610–11	*The Winter's Tale, The Tempest.* Shakespeare retires to Stratford.
1612–13	*Henry VIII, The Two Noble Kinsmen.*
1616	Marriage of daughter Judith on February 10. Shakespeare dies at Stratford on April 23.
1623	Publication of the Folio edition of Shakespeare's plays.

Contributors

HAROLD BLOOM, Sterling Professor of the Humanities at Yale University, is the author of *The Anxiety of Influence, Poetry and Repression,* and many other volumes of literary criticism. His forthcoming study, *Freud: Transference and Authority,* attempts a full-scale reading of all of Freud's major writings. A MacArthur Prize Fellow, he is general editor of five series of literary criticism published by Chelsea House. During 1987–88, he served as Charles Eliot Norton Professor of Poetry at Harvard University.

MARJORIE B. GARBER is Professor of English at Harvard University. She is the author of *Coming of Age in Shakespeare* and *Dream in Shakespeare: From Metaphor to Metamorphosis.*

MICHAEL NEILL is Senior Lecturer in English at the University of Auckland, and the author of numerous articles on Shakespeare. He is co-editor of the plays of John Marston.

MADONNE M. MINER teaches in the Department of English at the University of Wyoming. She is the author of *Insatiable Appetites: Twentieth-Century American Women's Bestsellers.*

JOHN W. BLANPIED is the author of *Time and the Artist in Shakespeare's English Histories.*

R. CHRIS HASSEL, JR., is Professor of English at Vanderbilt University. He is the author of *Faith and Folly in Shakespeare's Romantic Comedies* and *Renaissance Drama and the English Church Year* and is working on the New Variorum edition of *Richard III.*

MARGUERITE WALLER is Associate Professor of English and European Studies at Amherst College and the author of articles on Petrarch and Shakespeare, as well as *Petrarch's Poetics and Literary History.*

C. L. BARBER was Professor of Literature at the University of California at Santa Cruz. He wrote the influential *Shakespeare's Festive Comedy* and co-authored *The Whole Journey: Shakespeare's Power of Development.*

RICHARD P. WHEELER, Professor of English Literature, University of Illinois, Urbana, is the author of *Shakespeare's Development and the Problem Comedies* and co-author of *The Whole Journey: Shakespeare's Power of Development.*

Bibliography

Berry, Edward I. *Patterns of Decay: Shakespeare's Early Histories*. Charlottesville: University of Virginia Press, 1975.

Berry, Ralph. *"Richard III:* Bonding the Audience." In *The Mirror up to Shakespeare: Essays in Honour of G. R. Hibbard,* edited by J. C. Gray, Toronto: University of Toronto Press, 1984.

Boris, Edna Zwick. *Shakespeare's English Kings, the People and the Law*. Rutherford, N.J.: Associated University Presses, 1978.

Brooks, Harold F. *"Richard III,* Unhistorical Amplifications: The Women's Scenes and Seneca." *The Modern Language Review* 75 (1979): 721–37.

Burckhardt, Sigurd. *Shakespearean Meanings*. Princeton: Princeton University Press, 1968.

Burton, Delores M. "Discourse and Decorum in the First Act of *Richard III.*" *Shakespeare Studies* 14 (1981): 55–84.

Campbell, Lily B. *Shakespeare's Histories: Mirrors of Elizabethan Policy*. San Marino, Calif.: Huntington Library, 1947.

Champion, Larry S. "Myth and Counter-Myth: The Many Faces of Richard III." In *A Fair Day in the Affections: Literary Essays in Honor of Robert B. White, Jr.* Raleigh, N.C.: The Winston Press, 1980.

———. *Perspective in Shakespeare's English Histories*. Athens: University of Georgia Press, 1980.

Clemen, Wolfgang H. *A Commentary on Shakespeare's* Richard III. Translated by Jean Bonheim. London: Methuen, 1968.

Cluck, Nancy A. "Shakespearean Studies in Shame." *Shakespeare Quarterly* 36 (1985): 141–51.

Cutts, J. P. *The Shattered Glass: A Dramatic Pattern in Shakespeare's Early Plays*. Detroit: Wayne State University Press, 1968.

Dash, Irene G. *Wooing, Wedding, and Power: Women in Shakespeare's Plays*. New York: Columbia University Press, 1981.

Doebler, Bettie Anne. " 'Despair and Dye': The Ultimate Temptation of *Richard III.*" *Shakespeare Studies* 7 (1974): 75–85.

Driver, Tom F. *The Sense of History in Greek and Shakespearean Drama*. New York: Columbia University Press, 1960.

Dusinberre, Juliet. *Shakespeare and the Nature of Women*. London: Macmillan, 1975.

121

Faber, M. D. *The Design Within: Psychoanalytic Approaches to Shakespeare*. New York: Science House, 1970.

Fiedler, Leslie. *The Stranger in Shakespeare*. New York: Stein & Day, 1972.

Frey, David L. *The First Tetralogy: Shakespeare's Scrutiny of the Tudor Myth*. The Hague: Mouton, 1976.

Gupta, S. C. Sen. *Shakespeare's Historical Plays*. London: Oxford University Press, 1964.

Heilman, Robert B. "Satiety and Conscience: Aspects of Richard III." In *Essays in Shakespearean Criticism*, edited by James L. Calderwood and Harold E. Toliver. Englewood Cliffs, N.J.: Prentice-Hall, 1970.

Holland, Norman. *Psychoanalysis and Shakespeare*. New York: McGraw-Hill, 1966.

Kahn, Coppélia. *Man's Estate: Masculine Identity in Shakespeare*. Berkeley: University of California Press, 1981.

Kelly, Henry A. *Divine Providence in the England of Shakespeare's Histories*. Cambridge: Harvard University Press, 1970.

Kott, Jan. *Shakespeare Our Contemporary*. Translated by Boleslaw Taborski. Garden City, N.Y.: Anchor Books, 1966.

Lindenberger, Herbert. *Historical Drama*. Chicago: University of Chicago Press, 1975.

MacDonald, Andrew, and Gina MacDonald. "The Necessity of Evil: Shakespeare's Rhetorical Strategy in *Richard III*." *Shakespeare Studies* 19 (1980–81): 55–69.

Manheim, Michael. *The Weak King Dilemma in the Shakespearean History Play*. Syracuse, N.Y.: Syracuse University Press, 1973.

Muller, Wolfgang G. "The Villain as Rhetorician in Shakespeare's *Richard III*." *Anglia* 102 (1984): 37–59.

Ornstein, Robert. *A Kingdom for a Stage: The Achievement of Shakespeare's History Plays*. Cambridge: Harvard University Press, 1972.

Palmer, John. *Political Characters of Shakespeare*. London: Macmillan, 1961.

Pierce, Robert B. *Shakespeare's History Plays, the Family and the State*. Ohio: Ohio State University Press, 1971.

Prior, Moody. *The Drama of Power: Studies in Shakespeare's History Plays*. Evanston, Ill.: Northwestern University Press, 1973.

Rabkin, Norman. *Shakespeare and the Problem of Meaning*. Chicago: University of Chicago Press, 1981.

Ranald, Margaret Loftus. "Women and Political Power in Shakespeare's Histories." *Topic* 36 (1982): 54–65.

Reese, M. M. *The Cease of Majesty: A Study of Shakespeare's History Plays*. London: Edward Arnold, 1961.

Ribner, Irving. *The English History Play in the Age of Shakespeare*. London: Methuen, 1965.

Richmond, Hugh M. "*Richard III* and the Reformation." *Journal of English and Germanic Philology* 83 (1984): 509–21.

Righter, Anne [Anne Barton]. *Shakespeare and the Idea of a Play*. London: Penguin, 1967.

Rossiter, A. P. *Angel with Horns and Other Shakespeare Lectures*. Edited by Graham Storey. New York: Theatre Arts Books, 1961.

———"The Structure of *Richard III.*" *Durham University Journal* (1938–39).

Saccio, Peter. *Shakespeare's English Kings.* London: Oxford University Press, 1977.

Sanders, Wilbur. *The Dramatist and the Received Idea.* Cambridge: Cambridge University Press, 1968.

Shupe, Donald R. "The Wooing of Lady Anne: A Psychological Inquiry." *Shakespeare Quartely* 29 (1978): 28–36.

Siegel, Paul N. *Shakespeare's English and Roman History Plays: A Marxist Approach.* Rutherford, N.J.: Fairleigh Dickinson University Press, 1986.

Smidt, Kristian. *Unconformities in Shakespeare's History Plays.* London: Macmillan, 1982.

———. *Injurious Imposters and Richard III.* New York: Humanities Press, 1964.

Smith, Denzell S. "The Credibility of the Wooing of Anne in *Richard III.*" *Papers on Language and Literature* 7 (1971): 299–302.

Spivak, Bernard. *Shakespeare and the Allegory of Evil.* New York: Columbia University Press, 1958.

Thomas, Sidney. *The Antic Hamlet and Richard III.* New York: King's Crown Press, 1943.

Tillyard, E. M. W. *Shakespeare's History Plays.* London: Chatto & Windus, 1944.

Toole, William B. "The Motif of Psychic Division in *Richard III.*" *Shakespeare Survey* 27 (1974): 21–32.

Waith, Eugene M., ed. *Shakespeare: The Histories.* Englewood Cliffs, N.J.: Prentice-Hall, 1965.

Wheeler, Richard P. "History, Character and Conscience in *Richard III.*" *Comparative Drama* 5 (1971–72): 301–21.

Whitaker, Virgil K. *The Mirror up to Nature.* San Marino, Calif.: Huntington Library, 1965.

Wilders, John. *The Lost Garden.* London: Macmillan, 1978.

Wilson, F. P. "The English History Play." In *Shakespearean and Other Studies,* edited by Helen Gardner, 1–53. Oxford: Clarendon Press, 1969.

Winny, James. *The Player King: A Theme of Shakespeare's Histories.* New York: Barnes & Noble, 1968.

Acknowledgments

"Dream and Plot" (originally entitled "Apparent Prodigies") by Marjorie B. Garber from *Dream in Shakespeare: From Metaphor to Metamorphosis* by Marjorie B. Garber, © 1974 by Yale University. Reprinted by permission of Yale University Press.

"Shakespeare's Halle of Mirrors: Play, Politics, and Psychology in *Richard III*" by Michael Neill from *Shakespeare Studies* 8 (1975), © 1975 by the Council for Research in the Renaissance. Reprinted by permission.

" 'Neither Mother, Wife, nor England's Queen': The Roles of Women in *Richard III*" by Madonne M. Miner from *The Woman's Part: Feminist Criticism of Shakespeare,* edited by Carolyn Ruth Swift Lenz, Gayle Greene, and Carol Thomas Neely, © 1980 by the Board of Trustees of the University of Illinois. Reprinted by permission of the University of Illinois Press.

"The Dead-End Comedy of *Richard III*" by John W. Blanpied from *Time and the Artist in Shakespeare's English Histories* by John W. Blanpied, © 1983 by Associated University Presses, Inc. Reprinted by permission.

"Military Oratory in *Richard III*" by R. Chris Hassel, Jr., from *Shakespeare Quarterly* 35, no. 1 (Spring 1984), © 1984 by the Folger Shakespeare Library. Reprinted by permission of the *Shakespeare Quarterly*.

"Usurpation, Seduction, and the Problematics of the Proper: A 'Deconstructive,' 'Feminist' Rereading of the Seductions of Richard and Anne" by Marguerite Waller from *Rewriting the Renaissance: The Discourses of Sexual Difference in Early Modern Europe*, edited by Margaret W. Ferguson, Maureen Quilligan, and Nancy J. Vickers, © 1986 by the University of Chicago. Reprinted by permission of the University of Chicago Press.

"Savage Play in *Richard III*" (originally entitled "Savage Play and the Web of Curses in *Richard III*") by C. L. Barber and Richard P. Wheeler from *The Whole Journey: Shakespeare's Power of Development* by C. L. Barber and Richard P. Wheeler, © 1986 by the Regents of the University of California. Reprinted by permission of the University of California Press.

Index

127